Success With Meaning

Success With Meaning

First Edition

The 5 Proven Steps to Life with Success

Ernst Alahram Louis-Jacques

Action 5 Publishing

Sunrise

COPYRIGHT PAGE

Success with Meaning

Author: Ernst Alahram Louis-Jacques
Publisher: Action5 Publishing
ISBN: 979-8-9908339-0-6

Author's Disclaimer

I have carefully cited and referenced all the ideas, quotes, and concepts presented in this book. In the event that any idea or work is not properly credited, it is purely unintentional and an oversight on my part. I respect the intellectual property rights of others and will promptly rectify any such omission if brought to my attention. Please contact me with any concerns regarding proper attribution. My main intention throughout this book project is to make the world a better place.

NOTICE OF LIABILITY

CREDITS

Cover design and illustrations by: Chelsea St Cyr
Editing by: Chelsea St Cyr and Veronique Louis-Jacques
Consultants: Marion Weldon and Chelsea St Cyr

CONTACT INFORMATION

Action5 Publishing
9200 NW 53rd Street, Sunrise FL 33351
info@action5.com
action5publishing.com

Printed in the United States of America
First Edition: 2024

Dedication

To My Beloved Father, Andre Robert Louis-Jacques

Your life story has been my primary source of inspiration. Your strength, wisdom, and unconditional love guide me daily. This book is dedicated to you and represents a testament to the lessons you instilled in me, carrying forward your legacy of self-discipline, mission, courage, bravery, continuous learning, action, integrity, compassion, faith, and optimism. Though you are no longer with us, your spirit echoes through every page, and I am forever grateful for the foundation you laid for me.

To honor and sustain your mission of promoting education, I pledge 10% of all profits from this book to support educational projects, notably "Notre Dame of Lourdes Elementary School" in Leogane, Haiti. This school, which you supported during the last chapter of your life, will be prioritized when sharing these contributions from the book sales. It is a privilege to uphold this promise as a token of my love and admiration for you, ensuring that your mission continues to inspire and impact future generations.

With all my love and gratitude,
Your son,

Table of Contents

Foreword

Have you ever wondered why hard work often fails to produce the desired results in your life, school, or career? Have you set a New Year's resolution, only to fall short year after year? Do you struggle to stay focused, calm, and confident during stressful times, while others seem composed in similar situations? Does traditional personal development advice, like positive thinking, visualization, or habit tracking, feel more like pushing a boulder uphill rather than being effortless and motivating as things fall into place?

How do people find the time to give back to their community, serve others, and create a legacy? Is it possible to break free and choose the life you truly aspire to live?

The answer to these common personal development challenges lies in a factor often overlooked or minimized by most motivational authors and speakers: a factor that is entirely self-managed. In this transformative book, *Success with Meaning*, the author reveals a powerful model that will help you redesign your thinking, habits, and patterns to set you on a course for success. Ernst will guide you through every step of the process with his inspiring personal stories, which include ways to transcend fear, self-sabotage, and a sense of failure.

I first met Ernst Alahram Louis-Jacques, the remarkable author of this book, in 1993. He was one of twenty-two students from Central America and the Caribbean who earned scholarships to participate in a two-year Business Development Program at Edmonds Community College. At the time, I was the Department Chair and faculty instructor for the business management department, and knowing each of these students was a life-changing experience for me. Ernst brought a unique combination of personal qualities to this team. He was a few years older than most classmates, humble, funny, friendly, artistic, highly resourceful, and one of three motivated students from Haiti. In a short time, he inspired many campus community members through an unwavering sense of purpose and his mission-driven persona, which ultimately became his signature strength.

After Ernst's graduation in 1995, we lost contact. Miraculously, in 2023, through the wonders of social media, Ernst reached out. We exchanged updates, and I learned about his dream and how, thirty years earlier, he had taken a class assignment to an extraordinary new level. The assignment was based on Jack Canfield's program on Self-Esteem and Peak Performance. Ernst engaged with this ninety-minute video program more than twenty times, resonated deeply with its system, and set about creating his own unique model for success.

Fast-forward to 2024. Ernst is here to teach you how to discover your mission—an essential element that most motivational speakers and authors overlook. With mission and service at the core, he will teach you the MVP-PA model, showing you how to transform your finances, health, career, and relationships toward an impactful life. Over decades, Ernst has self-guided his own successes with this model and will teach you how to do the same in less time.

Through this book and accompanying workshops, you will access an education that empowers you to achieve consistent and sustainable results. Learn from a pro who will guide you every step of the way, helping you get the desired results by continuously raising the bar, setting new goals, and achieving success with meaning throughout your life. As Oprah once said, "Every person in the world has a purpose (mission) in life. No matter who you are, what you do, or how far you have already come, you have been tapped by a force greater than yourself to step into your calling. The work of your life is to figure out this calling."

Today is the day to embark on this transformative journey. Welcome Ernst Alahram Louis-Jacques into your life and let him show you how to navigate *success with meaning*.

Believing in you,

Marion

Marion Weldon (she/her)
Certified Career-Life Transformational Consultant

Preface

I am pleased to share a collection of personal stories enriched with educational and professional insights, from which I have drawn conclusions to develop a model for personal and professional success. In this context, success transcends personal achievement, encompassing innovation and actions that generate a long-lasting, positive impact on the world.

The MVP-PA model is designed to guide students, professionals, and entrepreneurs in pursuing success methodically without sacrificing their health, balance, and happiness. I intentionally avoided presenting this book as a research project. Instead, my life experiences and educational background—representing more than forty years of life enrichment—serve as the primary sources of inspiration.

My diverse roles as speaker, sales professional, business owner, writer, and artist converge on one unique mission: to enhance the human experience in personal development through my speeches, writings, artworks, and actions. This book reflects each facet of my personal and professional life. Over the past forty years, I have met over five thousand individuals who have shared their life experiences with me as I worked to solve their needs. These individuals, along with my instructors, parents, neighbors, classmates, and friends, have played a crucial role in my personal growth. It is an honor to share the valuable lessons I have learned from the people who have impacted my multifaceted life journey. Though I did not set out to conduct extensive research, the wealth of knowledge I gained during the writing process amazed me. I delved into concepts such as Ikigai, logotherapy, existential analysis, existentialism, SMART goals, SWOT analysis, and more to enrich the reading journey. I am glad that, in some way, I was able to incorporate the philosophy of my art style, which I call *"spiralism,"* into my writings.

As an artist, I consider myself a *spiralist. Spiralism* is a literary and artistic genre initially developed by three famous Haitian writers and artists. It uses spirals in artworks and writing, conveying messages through complex interactions of thought-provoking ideas, forms, themes, and thought structures. The most famous artist and writer associated with this genre is Frank Étienne, whose novels have been translated into English. Frank Étienne has a rich repertoire of paintings, books, and plays. He is known for his magnificent creativity, abundant production, and remarkable freedom of expression in art and writing.

However, my approach to *spiralism* differs significantly. I also use spirals, but my style's key philosophy is that no art project ever has a plan. I only have a key theme or model to illustrate for the final creation, just like authoring this book. I became an adventurer, searching for a dream island of artistic beauty, science, and wisdom. I did not have a rigid outline; the book takes its direction as we go along, just like in my paintings. I let my inspiration take over as if my intuition or a higher power guided me. I let Universal Intelligence guide the direction of the final work. You can never tell with certainty where life will take you, but you can be resolute about your achievements and your ability to transform any lemon given to you into delicious lemonade. Human life can be defined as a spiral, and the Universe, like nature, uses *spiralism* in its creation process.

The story about the $4 book, which I will share with you in the last chapter, illustrates my point about the spiral of life. In 1989, I bought a book titled *L'Art et le Vivant: Éveil à la Création* from a bookstore in Haiti. The title translates into English as *Art and Life: Awakening to Creation*. This book has remarkably shaped my personal and professional life. Today, I can proudly say I am a *spiralist*, even though my *spiralism* emerged from a French author, Georges Brunon, with no official ties to the *spiralist* genre, who advocates an approach that encourages readers to integrate bodily movements and spirals in their drawings. This fosters a synchronicity between the artist's body and the artwork during the creative process. This significantly influenced my artistic methods. Georges Brunon did not use the term *spiralism* or label it as an artistic genre even though he was using spirals, but I intuitively figured that I was using spirals and automatically became a *spiralist*. Surprisingly, Georges Brunon, a French painter and writer, helped me uncover a hidden treasure in my own backyard in Haiti—*Spiralism*. Originating in Haiti, Spiralism is a literary and artistic movement that uses spirals as the foundational motif to express feelings, emotions, ideas, and creativity. This approach not only enabled its founders to convey their thoughts and artistic visions safely but also allowed them to preserve their freedom of expression, serving as a creative refuge under a restrictive totalitarian regime.

This powerful book helped me discover the gifted artist within me. I was fortunate enough to transform the teachings of the

$4 book into a wonderful new way of painting. May the world greatly benefit from my artistic and literary creations.

What a subtle way to invite you, especially the new generations, to read and take action for lasting achievement, as reading has profoundly transformed my life.

I am convinced that teaching the MVP-PA success model will have some unintended results, especially in mental health. This was not my primary goal, but as my exploration of the model progressed, I realized that someone who clearly knows the purpose of their life while taking meaningful action whenever necessary will acquire the ability to minimize their mental health issues.

Many years ago, I decided to import organizational development principles into the personal development field to build personal achievement. An effective organization knows its mission and stays focused on it while connecting every member of the organization around the core principles of that mission. Similarly, if a person knows their mission and keeps an unwavering focus on it, they will likely find a balance in their life. I leave the research assignments to professionals in psychology and psychotherapy. However, I tend to compare myself to Sydney Banks, a ninth-grade welding professional who, in 1973, revolutionized the field of psychology. He discovered the three principles of mind, thought, and consciousness, usually called the "Three Principles Psychology" or "Three Principles Therapy." Sydney Banks and I could be compared as influencers with no initial authority or substantial knowledge in the field of psychology, as neither of us had formal training in the subject at the time of our realizations.

A laser-sharp focus on your life's purpose should have the potential to solve, at least partially, your mental health challenges. Dr. Viktor Frankl shed some light on the subject with his creation of logotherapy, a method used to heal psychotherapy patients by helping them find meaning in their lives. This remains a remarkable discovery: finding meaning and knowing your life's mission will eventually lead to personal balance and achievement.

I am grateful to my wife, whose insistence on producing a quality book has undoubtedly influenced my diligence in compiling information and finalizing the book. Additionally, this publication owes much to the support of two key contributors: Marion Weldon, my business management professor at Edmonds Community College in Lynnwood, Washington, from 1993 to 1995, whose guidance has shaped my inspiration and discussions over the past six months; and Chelsea St Cyr, my multifaceted book publishing coach, graphic designer, and editor-in-chief, whose expertise has been invaluable.

By incorporating diverse elements, readers will gain a comprehensive understanding of my approach to success, the importance of a personal mission that guides plans and projects, and the urgent need for meaningful action. I urge you to take full responsibility for your destiny and actively shape your future. In doing so, you should recognize the subtle presence of Universal Intelligence, which teaches us to be humble and receptive, complementing our efforts without defining them.

My heartfelt promise to you, the reader, is that this book will convey multiple lessons and stories you will cherish for a lifetime, serving as your golden keys to personal and professional achievement. Reading this book will contribute to building a better world. For further insights and resources on the success model, visit action5.com, where I engage in meaningful conversations and invite your participation.

Enjoy a transformative reading experience!

Introduction

Good morning,

What a stunning sunrise! I am greeting the sunshine in you
with excitement. Even if you read this at night, the morning
symbolizes a fresh start, a new beginning. Similarly, I am
greeting the sun in you that never sets. Amazingly, a
magnificent sun is inside you, constantly enlightening your
body and life. The sun rises every morning to provide enough
light to carry you through a challenging day. I sometimes
imagine that our human scalps are like thin solar panels,
energizing our brains day and night to activate our
productivity and maintain our health. It is something to
contemplate as you embark on this journey of *Success with
Meaning.* Isn't it wonderful that you receive this magnificent
sunlight unconditionally every day? Let that inspire you to
impact humanity and the universe positively.

You would admit that high school graduations generate great
satisfaction for parents, teachers, and students. Those
indescribable sentiments of excitement, fulfillment, and
achievement derive from the feeling of overcoming tons of
obstacles. For the same reason, these experiences awaken in
the students a sense of uncertainty concerning their future.
What a remarkable day in June 1989 in Port-au-Prince, Haiti,
at my high school! Exceptional graduation festivities were
marked with inspirational speeches from school principals,
teachers, and students. We had recognition awards, music

performances, and gala dinners, all with a sense of distinction and magnificence—eighty-three proud students, each with their own unique skills, talents, dreams, and aspirations.

Unfortunately, after a beautiful day of celebration, the students had to be prepared for the national exam to obtain their official high school diploma from the Department of Education in Haiti, my home country.

Gratefully, all the students from the class of 1989 passed their national exams and officially received their coveted high school diplomas—a source of considerable pride at the time. Those who passed had their names broadcast on a lengthy list by the public radio station, a significant honor. The senior year, equivalent to the first year of college in the US, is called the philosophy class. This title marked a distinction for those young men and women driven by the provocative question of what tomorrow holds for them.

Right after celebrating our success, we had to determine the next step. Being a high school graduate was not the destination but merely the end of one of many cycles. Only a few had the opportunity to study abroad, either because their parents were already living overseas or because their families could afford the excessive costs of studying abroad. Most of us hurried to join preparatory classes for entrance exams at the country's only public university. Those classes were managed and held by teachers who found a way to create a lucrative business out of the entrance exams at the state university, which is supposed to be highly competitive. This complex system allows me to appreciate the SAT test in America, which streamlines the process of college applications for high school graduates. Just imagine two thousand applicants vying for only one hundred spots at the business school of Haiti's State University. It then became crucial for every student to ensure they had all the necessary tools to be among the fortunate few. Unlike in the United States, where education can be quite expensive, the State University of Haiti is tuition-free; I paid only $35 per semester for my four-year program. I use the word fortunate because the hundred students selected were not always those with the highest grades. Some may have benefited from connections to state officials and school administrators. You really had to be at the top of your game to make it there on merit alone. Life can be brutal sometimes, but we must be strong enough to face obstacles. Imagine the first day of class after being selected as one of the fortunate few in a country where the future remains uncertain because the demand for jobs is quite high compared to the availability of employment opportunities. As first-year students, we carried an extensive list of questions, uncertainties, fears, pride, and satisfaction for making it there.

During that first week of class, I was fortunate to listen to my business math teacher, Mr. Theodat, who gave me one of the greatest gifts: recommendations for achieving professional success. Mr. Theodat advised us to acquire a mentor during our senior year at the university, suggesting that this would facilitate our entry into the job market and enhance our chances of success. I will share how this advice has benefited my professional life in one of the chapters of this book. This journey has brought me scholarships, job opportunities, friends, travel opportunities, multiple skill sets, and more.

Since then, many doors of opportunity have opened for me. The satisfying outcomes stem from a straightforward process I would like to share with everyone aspiring to maintain a fulfilled life experience. Once understood and implemented, this process will lead you to one destination: the top of the pyramid of achievement. I refer to this as the science of success because it transcends luck, offering instead a series of verifiable steps and procedures that will inevitably lead to personal accomplishment. If you adhere to the steps outlined here, you will achieve success with meaning, regardless of your education level, age, financial resources, or number of connections. As in every durable construction, the foundation is key to building a solid achievement pyramid.

The human experience represents an incredible and challenging journey. It is an adventure that is naturally attractive because we, as human beings, are endowed with the ability to transform our world through countless opportunities and unlimited potential. Indeed, humans have the power to dominate the world despite circumstances beyond our control. Given the abundance of possibilities and potential at our disposal, we can dare to dream of going to the moon and returning safely to Earth. If we can dream it, we can achieve it. Intentions that once seemed out of this world have now become tangible realities. Indeed, you and I can dream, imagine, and visualize the world we want to live in. We can take advantage of infinite possibilities and enjoy the abundant life we envision. The most significant realization is that the power of creation within us empowers us to design a life experience that truly reflects our unlimited capabilities. To the question, "Can you be successful?" you can undoubtedly answer, "Yes." Yes, you can be successful if you understand the process that leads to success—achieving your goals and transitioning toward improvement. Yes, you can be successful if you dream big enough. Yes, you can be successful if you take the time to explore all the talents and gifts you are equipped with—indeed, these are countless. Yes, you can be successful if you are willing to step out of your comfort zone and take the necessary actions to succeed. Yes, you can do it now, and I will accompany you on this journey through the quest for passion. Yes, you can do it if you stop contemplating why you cannot and instead act boldly to transform your personal and professional life positively.

I have been struck by the number of individuals seeking success yet struggling to grasp the journey. As a student and a business professional, I have cultivated a profound passion for achievement. For decades, I have immersed myself in the study of success, prioritizing the creation of a simple, actionable model that applies to students, college graduates, young professionals, public officials, and entrepreneurs alike. While the steps may require thoughtful consideration, once the intricacies of the process are understood, the prospect of crafting a mission-focused and prosperous career becomes attainable.

Successful people often employ simplification as a strategy to solve complex problems. They can effectively address and resolve challenges by breaking down complexities into manageable parts.

The marketplace is like a classroom, where the most successful students often avoid complicating the teacher's explanations. Simplification is a hallmark of successful and intelligent individuals because they streamline processes and problem-solving. A clear understanding of the steps involved in building success for us, our families, and those around us boosts our confidence and keeps us focused on our goals. It is important to note that I emphasize success that benefits others. Being successful is an act of love and personal responsibility; through our achievements, we create jobs, purchase more from entrepreneurs, and contribute more taxes, which the government can use to build and maintain public schools, hospitals, roads, and bridges. Thus, society always profits from your personal success.

Michael Bloomberg exemplifies this. In 2018, he donated 1.8 billion dollars from the proceeds of his success to Johns Hopkins University, thus becoming a champion in education by enabling the university to offer more grants and scholarships to undergraduate students. When you are successful, you can help build a better world. I encourage you to aim high, convinced that you possess the necessary qualities to be as successful as those who have reached the pinnacle of their fields.

 I desire to ignite within you a flame of passion for success, leading to fulfilling your life's mission. Our perception of life, the way we think, the quality of our interactions with others, our expectations, our attitudes, and our daily experiences all influence the outcomes of our lives. However, understanding the science or process of success can make achieving it more straightforward. Our discussion aims to ignite a burning passion for success, hot enough to burn away all obstacles and fears that prevent people from reaching their highest potential.

Many people have read countless books on success, subscribed to magazines about positive thinking, attended numerous seminars on personal development, and explored the habits of successful individuals, yet they have not taken action to make things happen in their own lives. You must aspire to manifest your incredible gifts and talents through significant actions that lead to remarkable accomplishments.

The journey with *success with meaning* will serve as a vibrant call for action.

The goal is clear: to ignite within you such a profound level of passion that you are driven to cultivate a culture of success. This culture of success will foster a passion that incites actions, transforming your dreams into reality. I invite you to be obsessed with success while maintaining a balance that keeps you healthy and happy.

The primary goal is to nurture a passion for personal and professional success within you. Once you develop a genuine love for achieving your mission, success will become inevitable, provided you consistently take action when necessary. I urge you to reflect and act on the ideas presented in the five magic steps to lifetime success: Mission, Vision, Passion, Plan, and Action, as you embark on this journey of positive transformation.

I have named this system the MVP-PA model. It embodies the five steps mentioned above and is a straightforward framework I designed to guide people toward achieving their dreams. Now, the big question for you is: Would you rather be a regular player or an MVP (Most Valuable Player) in the game of life?

If your answer is MVP, then the MVP-PA model should become your mantra. Rest assured, your commitment to applying the MVP-PA model will pave the way to personal success. This model is designed to inspire you to aspire to excellence in your professional and personal lives, opening the door to *success with meaning* and a focus on your primary mission.

I will share personal stories and lessons learned from teachers, friends, customers, and parents, incorporating insights I have cultivated over forty years. The following pages are designed to facilitate the connection between you and the champion or the MVP (Most Valuable Player) within you.

This journey aims to be a sunrise that enlightens you for a lifetime. Let's be ready to explore innovative ideas and concepts, a new way of thinking, and a new success model. Let's discover a basic model to help you climb the personal and professional achievement ladder. Let's explore what we really mean when we say *success with meaning*.

Part I

The Foundation of Success

Chapter 1
Success with Meaning: A New Approach to Success

"Strive not to be a success, but rather to be of value."[1]

– Albert Einstein

Have you ever been in a religious education class? These classes are typically boring for most students, but they rarely share these impressions with their parents. The good thing, cherished by all, is that they are easy to pass; everyone usually gets a passing grade. However, I fell in love with spirituality at an early age, which made me more inclined to listen to my religious education teachers. I consider one religious education class in high school to be among the most important classes I ever took. This was due to the invaluable lessons conveyed by my teacher, the late Father Claude Chenier, a Canadian missionary who devoted forty-six years of his life to educating children and adults in Haiti for faith, love, and

---

[1] Albert Einstein Quotes." BrainyQuote.com, BrainyMedia Inc, 2024. Accessed May 4, 2024.
https://www.brainyquote.com/quotes/albert_einstein_122232.

meaningful success. His teachings deeply resonated with me, and I took the time to listen and practice what he taught us. Father Chenier's dedication and teachings left a profound impact on me. He emphasized the importance of risk-taking, perseverance, compassion, empathy, and service to others.

His lessons instilled a deep sense of purpose and the drive to make a positive difference in the world. Father Chenier's class was not just an educational experience but a transformative journey that shaped my beliefs, values, and aspirations, aligning perfectly with the principles of "success with meaning." His mentorship, life story, and teachings illustrated the essence of "Personal Responsibility" and all the steps found in the MVP-PA success model.

1Success with Meaning, an Eternal Light for the World

Father Claude Chenier taught us to distinguish between "succeeding in life" and "fulfilling one's life." According to his teachings, succeeding in life is marked by personal accomplishments such as professional status, real estate assets, bank accounts, pension funds, investment accounts, power status, popularity, and so on. In contrast, fulfilling one's life involves positively impacting other people's lives or achieving a project that impacts the world positively. If our leaders, both in the private and public sectors, viewed success as improving the lives of others, we would have better workplaces, communities, and a better world.

Greta Thunberg is a perfect example. At just sixteen years old, this Swedish climate activist addressed the United Nations General Assembly in 2018 and 2019, highlighting the urgent climate change problems the world is facing.[2] Owning a multi-million-dollar house on the beach can never compare to Greta's accomplishments. She has already led a fulfilled life. Success is such a great concept; it has different meanings for different people and cannot be limited to a nice house on the beach or a few million dollars in the bank.

The power of transformation embodies success. You can rightfully claim success when you can convert your initial resources into an extraordinary new set of assets. True success lies in your capacity to multiply your resources exponentially. While I wholeheartedly encourage you to excel in your profession or venture into multi-million-dollar endeavors,

---

[2] BBC News. "Greta Thunberg: The Swedish Teen Who Became the Voice of Climate Change Activism." BBC News, December 11, 2019. Accessed May 17, 2024. https://www.bbc.com/news/world-europe-50740324.

I implore you to recognize that your potential extends beyond meeting personal needs. Within each of us resides a formidable and ingenious giant awaiting discovery. This ingenious giant can be harnessed to make the world a better place.

What if we could discover a formula capable of fostering success on two fronts: personal achievement and societal contribution? This is not an unrealistic notion; each of us has the potential to attain both personal success and genuine philanthropy. We can pursue our own aspirations while simultaneously uplifting thousands of lives. By striking a balance between serving the world and fulfilling our needs, we can achieve the dual objectives of personal success and meaningful impact, embodying what we call *success with meaning*.

I was fascinated one day by a conversation I had with Stephanie, my wife's niece, at our kitchen table in 2019. She mentioned that Christopher, her older brother, discussed the correct definition of a dream with her. According to Christopher, "A dream that does not affect other people's lives is not a dream." To him, when you think of something—big or small—for yourself, it is just a personal project or a simple desire.

This is another way to say that true success is defined by the amount of people that you have helped throughout your lifetime. If I apply Christopher's theory of dreams, becoming a doctor to be financially secure is a personal project, and becoming a doctor to save thousands of lives is a noble dream. Personal success and wealth are great, but we can do better. If you give me a nice house on the beach, I will gladly take it, but saving thousands of lives or helping the children of the world or your neighborhood to succeed in life and eventually fulfill their lives is far greater than just a multi-million-dollar house on the beach.

I invite you to reflect on Christopher's recommendation and dream with a higher purpose beyond just achieving personal success. The good thing about dreaming with a higher purpose is that we will end up being personally successful because people always respond to positive motivation and energy. Many people have become successful because they have thought of making a difference in other people's lives. This kind of motivation will attract positive people in your environment and people will feel that positive magnet when they are around you. The more people you attract, the easier it will be for you to reach your life's goals, and this will translate into success in the marketplace. Your positive aspirations and your willingness to help the world move forward will be expressed in all aspects of your life. That will bring personal success to you even if that is not your primary motivation. By wanting to make a difference in the world, you have ordered all the forces in the universe to operate with you. Your true and altruistic motivation will facilitate accomplishing your goals if you are enthusiastic about your aspirations and willing to take action to transform dreams into reality. You cannot lose if you work to make a difference in other people's lives. I do not suggest that you feel obligated to help everyone who approaches you, but your goal should be to succeed in life and contribute to making the world a better place.

During my conscious life experiences in the past forty years, I have realized that improving other peoples' lives leads to personal and professional success, which we all tend to pursue first. If your dream, as Christopher has mentioned to Stephanie, is to make a positive difference in other people's lives, you will take care of your egocentric needs anyway. To make a big dream come true, you cannot make it alone. You will need to build a network of people that can help you. And those people incidentally will also be helping you make it in life even though that was not your primary intention.

I have a few ideas I would like to share with you before we get to the core of our journey. We need to revisit the essential elements of success to explore and fully act on its principles. I will share my viewpoint on success and attempt to define some concepts for the purpose of my journey with you.

Personal Success Reimagined

Your personal success should be defined solely by you. However, it is important to prepare yourself for a decent life. There are a few concepts on which we need to find common ground. If you cannot satisfy your basic needs for food and security, it will be tough to live life fully. You do not need to be a millionaire or have a six-figure income to be considered successful, but you do need to create conditions for financial stability because living decently requires money. Success should not be measured by the amount of money and material things you possess; instead, it should be defined by your ability to live the life of which you have dreamed.

Some people make it all about money and end up with all the problems in the world. Have you heard about the mid-life crisis? This can be triggered by realizing that you have been wrong in chasing money and status all your life and that happiness is distancing itself from you as the money and status grow. Money is important, but it is not everything. If the goal is only to make money, I can be confident that you will be disappointed at some point. You should be clear on what your personal success looks like and not let other people or society define it for you. How you answer the question regarding your personal success will determine the steps you need to take to make that a reality.

Wealth should never be used to measure success, as it often results from being in the right place at the right time and making the right investment. I recall a story about an investor who realized he was a millionaire years later after investing in a startup company in Seattle, whose stock skyrocketed. Some people are wealthy, but they are not necessarily successful.

When comparing a successful coach to an MVP in the NBA, many people might think the MVP is more successful. The MVP receives more recognition and is idolized as the #1 player. However, the coach has a greater impact in terms of the number of players they can transform for impactful achievement. Isn't it very thought-provoking to consider that coaches, teachers, professors, and medical professionals at various levels are remarkably successful, even though they earn much less compared to many high-paid positions, such as those in professional sports? Players in professional sports make much more than teachers and professors, for example, simply because teachers cannot reach millions of children at once, whereas sports performances entertain millions of individuals in a single game, thereby bringing in more revenue. The difference is based on the revenue generated by the different lines of work. Great successes are found in all professions, and we, as members of society, should honor those individuals who are devoting their lives to the well-being of humanity regardless of their financial status.

Success with Meaning: Your Life Is a Gift to Humanity.

Success with meaning is personal success guided by a mission to improve the world. The best way to grasp the concept of *success with meaning* is to appreciate the idea of giving within the dynamic interactions of the universe, especially on our planet. It begins with the understanding that you are not alone. Everything in the universe is interconnected, and each action can impact the world's well-being, either positively or negatively. *Success with meaning* is rooted in love, demonstrated through the intrinsic value of personal responsibility. It manifests in a personal mission and purposeful actions that strive to make our community—and the world—a better place daily. I was inspired to connect success with the nature and power of giving in my attempt to define success as a means of reaching our personal goals while positively impacting the world.

You did not pay a dime to be alive. You came free of charge to yourself. Life has given you oxygen, water, a powerful brain, a miraculous body, parents, relatives, governments, schools, neighbors, and friends. At some point, you may think your life is yours, but it is not. Anything you do will profit or hurt the world; without that mindset, you have no choice but to be miserable. Your happiness will start the day you understand that you are a gift to the world. The more you give, the more you will receive. This last statement about giving sounds simple, but you can easily assess it. In the morning, if you greet everyone with a smile, you will almost certainly get a smile back. The remarkable thing about that simple smile is that it will help you make friends. Consequently, you will be able to learn more, grow, and become a better person. Unfortunately, many people have been wired wrongly and think that the more they take, the better off they will be.

The secret of success and balance is in the giving. Giving is not only about money. Giving can be in time, teaching, helping people with disabilities, and helping build a better society. I know a group of friends who created an organization to provide services to their compatriots in America. They have done this for about thirteen years without expecting personal gain, and they never planned to get a return. However, they have received a hundredfold return through a new business opportunity that arose from their efforts.

When someone commits suicide, they do not lose anything; rather, the world loses a valuable provider of knowledge, wisdom, time, and tremendous effort. When you die, you do not really lose. The losers are your parents, your friends, your co-workers, your company, your school, your support group, or your fraternity. At the end of the day, everything you do will go to someone else. That is why you need to do an excellent job. You want to leave something special and valuable for humanity. If you do not protect your life, you are doing a disservice to the world, not really to yourself. To grasp the concept, you need to think of the great personalities you have studied at school, such as Einstein, Gandhi, Nelson Mandela, Edison, Alexander Graham Bell, Toussaint Louverture, and so many other inventors and leaders. Because they wanted to leave something valuable to the world, they were able to enjoy success. Until today, the formula remains the same: the more you want to give, the more you will receive. Successful people are those who have decided to provide more than the average person, and, in return, they have received tremendous success. I want you to keep reading, but I am convinced I have shared a great secret of success with you. By giving, and giving more to the world, you will automatically create the conditions for your success.

It might be difficult for a human being to grasp the concept of a gift. Our ego can prevent us from understanding that this life does not really belong to us. I wish animals could talk, and they would be able to lecture us, human beings, on the concept of life as a gift to others. If you visit a forest or a farm, you will understand that everything is a gift to humanity. Everything in the forest is to be used by a member of the human species. The honeybees[3] are an example; they have a noticeably short lifespan, but their lives benefit humanity. They play a significant role in vegetation. Without bees, agriculture, which has been feeding humankind for thousands of years, would be paralyzed. The bees' lives clearly represent some of the gifts used to sustain human lives. It is reported that the queen bees live between one and two years, and the workers live on average fifteen to thirty-eight days during the summer and between 150 and 200 days during the winter. In effect, they have a short lifespan, but they carry such a heavy responsibility related to the welfare of humans.

---

[3] Remolina, Silvia C., and Kimberly A. Hughes. "Evolution and Mechanisms of Long Life and High Fertility in Queen Honeybees." Proceedings of the National Academy of Sciences of the United States of America 105, no. 9 (2008): 3461-3466. Accessed June 4, 2024. https://www.ncbi.nlm.nih.gov/pmc/articles/PMC2527632/.

Those disciplined workers conduct their mission as expected; you, too, should be committed to taking care of your mission. The main difference between a human being and a bee is that the bee is already programmed to perform a specific function, but the human being must make a choice among thousands of possibilities. It is already programmed in the bees' DNA to do that particular pollination job, and it does it so gracefully and intelligently. Every animal has its unique function to perform, and all do it as planned and let human beings take advantage of the gifts of their lives. If you know you are a gift to humanity, your life will be an enjoyable experience, and the world will benefit from it. The best thing is that nobody will have to lie at your funeral, saying that you were a great person when, in fact, you were not. Funerals are events where people lie a lot because I have never seen a eulogy that says: "The dead body in the casket hosted an unbelievably bad human being." The world will truly honor your presence.

It is all about *success with meaning. Success with meaning* remains the expression of outstanding performance through a personal mission aimed at helping the world become a better place, making a difference in people's lives, and understanding that giving, especially giving your best, is a requirement for lasting achievement.

Success Through Service and Legacy

Each one of us is searching for a mission in life. Whether you are eighteen or older, you are looking for a way to achieve balance, personal and financial success, and happiness. The mission is what brings value to you, and it is also the value that you bring to the world.

When someone does not know their mission, life becomes senseless. I believe that many cases of suicide, if not attached to mental illness or depression, stem from a lack of purpose or mission—or the belief that we are failing in our mission. Without a defined purpose, it is hard to experience great satisfaction in life because there is no benchmark for measuring your results.

Your mission, goals, and objectives are the tools you use to evaluate your actions introspectively. How you evaluate yourself, considering your values, directly correlates with your personal mission. Without a personal mission or purpose, you tend to go by other people's values and benchmarks.

With your mission as your compass, you can determine if you are on the right track at any moment of your life. Your actions will make sense when supported by a well-defined mission that you internalize daily or breathe as part of your existence. Knowing your mission is the beginning of a balanced and productive life.

Imagine yourself on a highway with no clear destination. You will feel lost because you have no fixed destination, and it will be easy to have an accident. We should consider our lives as vehicles on the highways of the world. We are the drivers of life vehicles, and it is imperative that we set our destinations.

It may sound easy to live without purpose, eat, drive, sleep, and have fun until death. However, this life will be viewed as a complete loss of treasure. No human being should ever live on this planet with no clear mission or destination because we are the only entity capable of affecting the course of planet Earth and eventually becoming a bigger part of the universe.

We can manipulate every other entity to produce and generate more value but cannot change the course of nature or the planet. It is our duty to do more to improve the earth and fix issues that need to be resolved. That is why it is so crucial for everyone to define their mission clearly.

We are born not just to breathe, grow, and die but to participate in resolving world issues. We should consider ourselves as gifts to humanity. However, our gifts will only be helpful if we reap the benefits of our lives through some improvement missions for the world.

If you know your true mission and understand that you are a gift to humanity, you will do your best to protect your life. Parents safeguard their lives within a family because they know their children's success and balance depend on it. On a larger scale, we indirectly preserve the world when we protect our own lives.

When we know and protect our missions, we can build our happiness, balance, and success. In doing so, we help maintain the world's balance. If we understand the power of our brains, we will realize how valuable we are to the world. We are the world's lights, the species that bears the greatest responsibility for improving planet Earth, and we must take that responsibility seriously.

Nowadays, we talk a lot about climate change, and many people have concluded that it is our responsibility to protect the planet by reducing the activities that negatively affect it. And it is not just about climate change; there are many issues that we must address as humans if we choose to survive and keep our race alive.

You may not have thought of your life this way, but you are also responsible for the welfare of our planet. You should not feel that it is only the responsibility of the leaders to keep the world balanced. It is your responsibility, too. By taking your personal responsibility regarding world balance, you reduce the pressure on the rest of the world. By being responsible individually, we simplify the task of building a better world.

You and I can build a majestic world; we need to identify our missions clearly to take daily actions accordingly. Anyone who clearly knows the content of their mission and commits to it has acquired the ticket to a successful and balanced life.

Achieving Professional Balance Through Personal Balance

As an insurance agent, I held sales seminars in North Miami Beach, Florida, with a team member named Lana. She was a great partner because she complemented me very well due to her fluency in Spanish and Russian. Besides English, I spoke French and Creole. Her ability to speak two other languages made us a powerful team for the South Florida market. When we held a seminar, we were almost certain that we would make at least one sale if people showed up because we spoke the languages of South Florida.

On top of our language skills, we are both very energetic and incredibly positive about the outcomes of our efforts. While preparing for a seminar, I asked Lana about her production for the month and business in general. She gave me an answer I will remember for the rest of my life: "Business is good because my personal life is good too." It is a straightforward statement that means so much in content. By saying that, Lana affirmed that personal life is the foundation for a successful and balanced professional life.

Have you realized that a good day at work starts with a good day at home? If you have subordinates at your job, they can easily know when things are working well at home. You are usually more approachable when things are going well at home. When the spouse gives that little reassuring kiss or says goodbye with a little "Have a great day, honey," they prepare you for the unexpected and challenging moments.

You are more creative, positive, and tolerant when things go well at home. On the contrary, if you leave home after a negative event involving your children or spouse, your outcomes for the day will automatically change. You become grumpier, and the people around you will have difficulty collaborating with you.

Your professional results are better when your personal life is better. If we look deeper, we will find the reasons why a balanced personal life maintains a balanced professional life. You are more joyful; this joy builds a positive aura around you. People will want to collaborate with you because they want some of that joy, consciously or unconsciously. They want that natural smile that you do not need to force.

You are more creative; the brain works better when you are emotionally balanced. You are more responsive and inclined to generate innovative ideas if the job requires a brainstorming session. You are more tolerant; your teammates are more comfortable working with you. If someone has a question, you take your time to respond, and you are naturally polite. With unhealthy emotions, you rush to blame or give quick answers because you do not want to deal with the inconvenience of uncertainty.

Your Contributions Are Unique

You are not in a race. As we go through life, it is easy to think that it is a race in which we must compare ourselves with others. Sometimes, we make other people's accomplishments our benchmarks, but our lives are unique, and we should always consider ourselves a unique castle in the world. It is okay to have a role model, someone who inspires you to discover this wonderful part of yourself whose only desire is to grow a better you. Therefore, the role model is not someone you are in a race with. The role model represents your inspiration for greatness. We complement each other in many ways, and that is what makes the world great. No profession is better than another; no mission is less important if the intent is to solve a human or societal problem or need. How your mission is delivered depends entirely on your decisions and how you want to carry it out.

You should measure your success by personal accomplishments aligned with your well-defined mission, not by society's benchmarks. I personally like prominent properties and extraordinary amounts of money. However, I know that a successful life is expressed in more than a fat bank account. How many people are both miserable and filthy rich? How many people do not know what to give for a healthy and balanced life? Have you seen those with massive houses and more bedrooms than they need, yet they do not have the time to enjoy them or must sacrifice their health to maintain that lifestyle?

I will always ask you to dream big; it benefits humanity. Your big dreams will create jobs and help humanity solve hunger, health, security, and many other issues. It is best to find a balance between your wealth and your health to avoid life becoming senseless and driving you to depression or any other types of crises. I have seen many parents put their children in a race that those children did not set for themselves, and those races set by parents most often result in disappointments and frustrations on both sides. When you want your kids to be #1 in a particular sport or discipline, they will make it to the MVP status only if they have embraced your goals as their own. At some point in their lives, they must personally choose to become number one and famous in the discipline you suggested for them.

A personal roadmap should never be chosen as a function of what society wants or aspires to. As a unique entity with potential, you must clearly understand your uniqueness and define your roadmap to success and greatness. Greatness lives in you and awaits to be uncovered. You can change the course of the world. This ability can never be fully explored if you see yourself in someone else's shoes. You must own your personal definition of life, your own goals, your chosen roadmap, your life's mission, your designed plan, your vision, your personal dreams, your personal projects, actions, and initiatives.

If you consider yourself part of a race for greatness, you must run daily in sight of your mission. If you care for your mission and purpose, you should be at peace with yourself. Our role is not to follow other people's actions, even if we can pick someone as a role model.

Thinking about your uniqueness makes you understand why taking care of your mission is so important. Nobody can perform your personal mission in your place. Each one should keep in mind that they are irreplaceable. That mission is to be approved by you and executed by you only. You can ask other people for help, but at the end of the day, you are the CEO of your life's enterprise. You have the sole responsibility for making your mission a reality.

Your Success Highway and Its Workers

You will encounter diverse types of support on your way to success in life. As I have always mentioned to people around me, success will not just happen to you; it is a process that requires the support of many contributors.

Do you have people you can contact for advice and recommendations when making important decisions? What about role models? Do you have people who inspire you to discover your best self?

Life is like a regular profession, even though it runs 24/7 compared to a typical profession. In any profession, there is an apprenticeship for aspiring professionals. During an apprenticeship, you model the expert to whom you are exposed. While it may not be as clear-cut, the apprenticeship model can be applied throughout your life. Some people hold the secret to success by applying themselves to life or through their natural choices. Either way, those people can be followed, much like influencers on social media. When making decisions, you can ask yourself how that role model would behave in your situation or, if possible, reach out to them for advice. You should never be afraid to ask. If you have access to role models, they are no longer just role models; these resource people are also your mentors. Mentors play two roles when used effectively: they become your advisors and serve as role models.

The movie industry can be used to provide those role models by displaying excellent characters who display problem-solving skills and life approaches that can be duplicated for the success of younger generations. Every person should have a frame of reference for their success in handling professional matters and personal life issues.

I will remember Professor Theodat from my first college experience for the rest of my life. During his first presentation to the business math class, he introduced the concept of a mentor as a ticket to success. He advised everyone to get themselves a mentor in their senior year of college. A mentor, by definition, represents someone with the status of an accomplished professional in your field of study and can help you climb the ladder of success. During my trajectory as a student, I applied his advice as specified, and it worked for me like a charm. In making your life a success, a mentor holds incredible value in building your skills, especially your life skills. Remember that success resembles a large door that just one person cannot open. To be incredibly successful in making a difference and building personal accomplishments, you must count on other people's input, influence, and contributions.

When I entered the insurance industry in 2008 as a sales agent, my initial attitude did not work for me. My results changed drastically after conversing with a manager who represented both a role model and a mentor. I am thankful to have been exposed to him and his advice. He is a big contributor to my success as a sales agent. One day, I went to him and explained that I thought I was too sophisticated for the position and was not making an effective connection with the prospects. He coached me that day, and since then, I acquired the attitude necessary to be successful in the profession.

As you can see, your mentor remains someone who can design a roadmap for your success. They are meant to impact your career similarly, and these roles can be labeled differently: heroes, mentors, role models, and coaches. It is important to note that your parents can also play those roles. My dad was my hero, and I learned much from him to build my success.

Wealth Is not a Sin nor Unethical

Finally, regarding success with meaning, I want to ensure that you do not consider wealth a sin or an obstacle to your ethical aspirations. Raised in a Christian environment, I have often encountered the presumption that being wealthy is prohibited or considered a deviation from God. Many people think that wealth makes individuals unethical. However, attitude can be everything. It is vital to change this mindset because if one believes that wealth is inherently wrong, they might never allow themselves to pursue or attain it. It is ok to be wealthy.

I raise this point because I am convinced that while some people have the ability to be wealthy, they may believe that desiring riches is not normal for believers or that God does not want people to be rich. Knowing that no one can live in contradiction to their subconscious beliefs, it will be nearly impossible for these individuals to experience wealth.

Some people believe that if they can meet their basic needs, they should not desire more or ask God for more, often out of fear of appearing greedy. However, I do not see desiring more as a problem. The issue arises when someone desires everything for themselves and nothing for others, even when others have contributed. It becomes problematic if you prioritize building your happiness solely around acquiring massive wealth. Instead of making wealth your primary objective, consider making fulfillment your aspiration. It's perfectly acceptable to dream of more and aspire to achieve tremendous success in life. Personally, I embrace the idea of more because I believe that the more you have, the more you can contribute to building a better world.

I have had numerous conversations with my son, Karl-Stephane, and one of these discussions centered on achieving substantial success. I conveyed to him that the willingness to exert considerable effort for significant success reflects love, as notable personal achievements benefit others and generate additional job opportunities. Conversely, individuals with modest ambitions can only satisfy their needs with limited resources. If you nurture big dreams, pursue a meaningful mission, and dedicate yourself to serving the world with honesty, integrity, and professionalism—while taking personal responsibility for yourself and society with a long-term vision—you will embody success with meaning.

My goal is to help you discover and achieve your mission in life while pursuing success with meaning. The purpose is to identify the steps needed to define a personal mission and recognize its importance. You will learn to set a vision, build passion, and craft a plan that will enable you to accomplish your mission and take the necessary steps to make it happen.

Read on to learn how to achieve your mission in life and become one of the MVPs (Most Valuable Players) on the planet through your uniqueness, discipline, forethought, and creative ability. In the next chapter, we will explore the concept of personal responsibility, which serves as the bedrock of the MVP-PA model presented in this book as the steps toward personal success, especially success with meaning.

Chapter 2
Personal Responsibility

"The price of greatness is responsibility."[4]

– Winston Churchill

I share Churchill's view on the fundamental connection
between greatness and responsibility. Responsibility is indeed
the price of achieving both greatness and success. In exploring
success with meaning, personal responsibility is crucial.
People naturally establish a foundation of personal
responsibility when searching for meaning in their lives.
Embracing positive psychology, which involves taking the
initiative to improve one's well-being and outlook, clearly
expresses this responsibility. By focusing on the positive
aspects of life's events, we demonstrate personal
responsibility, enhancing our character and benefiting society
at large.

---

[4] Winston Churchill Quotes. BrainyQuote.com, BrainyMedia Inc, 2024.
https://www.brainyquote.com/quotes/winston_churchill_101477, accessed
April 9, 2024

2Personal Responsibility: The World's Progress Depends on You Too

Since adopting the principle of personal responsibility at age ten, I have consistently seen its vital role in shaping success. Success is deeply tied to this concept, as every successful person has embraced it at some stage. Ultimately, those who achieve success are the ones who take control of their lives. Without a commitment to personal responsibility, achieving anything of value is highly challenging. When faced with obstacles, you must avoid blaming others and take ownership of every situation you encounter. This approach positions you to achieve favorable outcomes. By taking full responsibility for every aspect of your life, you will meet and exceed your expectations, ensuring your success is sustainable.

Definition of Personal Responsibility

As an insurance agent, having met over five thousand individuals at their retirement age, I am continually impressed by those who share that they dedicated thirty-five years to the same company without ever being late or missing a day, except for scheduled vacations. These individuals exemplify an exceptional degree of personal responsibility. For them, responsibility is inherently part of their identity; they approach every task with a personal commitment shown as a hallmark of their character.

Ron Haskins outlines that personal responsibility is intimately connected to societal norms: 'Personal responsibility is the willingness to accept the significance of standards that society sets for individual behavior and to exert considerable effort to abide by these standards.'[5] Yet, I view personal responsibility as critical in our journey toward personal growth. It is essential to manage every aspect of your life competently. In personal development, you must account for everything that happens in your life. Consequently, personal responsibility is the profound obligation to oneself regarding personal welfare and growth. This duty entails taking thorough care of oneself in every facet—guaranteeing responsibility for all personal outcomes. Hence, one should not blame external influences or

---

[5] Haskins, Ron. "The Sequence of Personal Responsibility." Brookings. Accessed [April 11, 2024]. https://www.brookings.edu/articles/the-sequence-of-personal-responsibility/#:~:text=Personal%20responsibility%20is%20the%20willingness,to%20live%20by%20those%20standards.

people, such as parents, friends, colleagues, or random events. Although environmental variables can impede your plans, a robust commitment to personal responsibility equips you to face any challenge life may pose. You are responsible for evaluating your circumstances, pinpointing areas needing enhancement, and pursuing effective remedies. The essential connection to personal responsibility is unmistakable in discussions about personal achievement. Individuals who find success frequently demonstrate this quality of personal responsibility. It manifests as a culture of self-dedication to doing the right thing, thus ensuring personal success, balance, and happiness. Ultimately, this commitment to personal responsibility also protects the broader society. When people fully embrace responsibility for their success and happiness, the entire community gains significantly. The practice of personal responsibility evolves into social responsibility. By attending to your own needs, you indirectly safeguard the community. A societal standard of personal responsibility naturally nurtures social stability.

Importance of Personal Responsibility

I am delighted to give personal responsibility a special place in exploring the concept of success, especially success with meaning. It allows me to understand the crucial value of personal responsibility and its significant role in keeping society on the right path. Many major religions emphasize love to encourage their followers to treat others fairly. However, it could be even more practical to focus the rule of conduct on the value of personal responsibility. If everyone takes their personal responsibility seriously, society can take advantage of the stability and growth that personal responsibility brings to everyone.

We can try to idealize the theme, but we meet personal responsibility daily. I know many parents who did not have a chance to enjoy their personal life simply because they felt responsible for their children's success. Therefore, they worked extremely hard to have enough money to send their children to the best schools. Sometimes, they would accept humiliation from bosses and customers to make their children successful. Those are classic examples of personal responsibility.

Personal responsibility manifests in various contexts: a child prioritizing study over pleasure to bring home good grades, a mayor rejecting bribes from special interest groups to ensure the well-being of residents, a president making decisions that benefit the majority rather than personal or close associates' success, and a teacher dedicated to providing the right education for students. Each example demonstrates the importance of prioritizing ethical behavior and accountability across distinct roles and responsibilities.

 I once met a successful journalist who shared an inspiring story during a presentation. He talked about how tough it was for his mother growing up, as she struggled to care for him and his siblings. Despite the hardships, her resilience and dedication played a significant role in shaping his path to success. He committed himself to ensuring that his mother would live in a decent home once he became successful. As soon as he got a well-paid position, he secured a nice house for her, demonstrating personal responsibility.

Similarly, I know a business owner with a comparable story. Raised in the Bahamas as a Haitian child, he witnessed his mother's sacrifices and promised to buy her a house when he could. A kindhearted American missionary adopted him, bringing him to the United States. After finishing high school and attending technical school for small engine repairs, he saved diligently from his earnings to fulfill his promise. Eventually, he bought his mother a house—a vivid demonstration of personal responsibility and dedication.

Three key institutions are pivotal in nurturing children's well-being and ensuring their safe upbringing in society: Families, churches, and schools. These institutions must always prioritize personal responsibility. Suppose parents begin teaching their children the concept of personal responsibility from an early age. In that case, they will better safeguard the future of their upbringing because personal responsibility emphasizes work over pleasure. The ideal aspiration of parents should center on inspiring their children to value work more than pleasure. Personal responsibility involves always doing the right thing. It compels us to think twice before acting, prompting us to ask ourselves: 'Is this the right thing to do?' Since 'right' might not necessarily relate to morality, we can reframe the question as: 'Is this a responsible thing to do?' The other day, I talked with a friend about high school graduates who have decided not to attend college. We concluded that deciding not to attend college is acceptable only if the graduates have a responsible plan for caring for their lives. A responsible member of society understands that the best way to be responsible is to have a profession that allows them to meet their needs by offering services to the community. Being your own boss is rewarding, but becoming an expert in at least one discipline or profession is crucial. Expertise will give you an edge in the marketplace. Society rewards individuals who possess the right skills. Although some irresponsible employers may exploit workers by underpaying them, having a profession is a critical step toward financial stability and freedom.

Without professional qualifications, individuals are more likely to be limited to low-paying jobs. Training to acquire a robust skill set increases one's marketability, opening doors to well-paying jobs and opportunities to thrive as an entrepreneur or independent contractor. I know individuals who might not be considered the brightest yet have achieved financial stability through personal responsibility and dedication to learning a trade or profession. When you are personally responsible, employers will value you, customers will seek your services, and your family will appreciate your presence.

Personal responsibility is crucial because it promotes self-care. When you are personally responsible, you tend to use your time efficiently and continually learn new skills to remain in high demand in the marketplace.

Churches must consistently teach personal responsibility. Love is inherently spiritual, but personal responsibility can be seen as love in action. When someone genuinely loves their neighbors, they feel compelled to protect them. This principle is applicable whenever one wishes to demonstrate love towards an individual or a group. Personal responsibility represents a profound and tangible expression of the spiritual principle of love for one another.

For instance, if a child genuinely loves their parents, this love might manifest in their efforts to be self-disciplined or display acceptable behaviors when interacting with others. Committing to be a team member in the household is also an expression of personal responsibility. Personal responsibility acts as the currency of collective or social stability, essential for maintaining harmony within the community.

Schools must consistently teach and reinforce the concept of personal responsibility until every child understands its importance. Teachers need to show children the value of discipline and teamwork. The school must maintain a culture that promotes discipline, hard work, mutual respect, cooperation among children, responsibility toward society, and respect for the environment. Schools must play their role in practicing the principles of personal responsibility.

Personal responsibility remains a profound and tangible expression of the spiritual principle of love for life and love for one another.

To be successful, the first step is embracing personal responsibility. Staying focused is crucial, and the principles of the MVP-PA success model provide the necessary tools to build that focus. Personal responsibility is one of the cornerstones of success; successful individuals are inherently responsible. It promotes good habits, such as going to bed early to ensure punctuality at school or work. It teaches moderation in leisure activities, like limiting TV watching to brief periods, except during vacations. Moreover, personal responsibility involves setting priorities effectively, such as choosing work over pleasure in a balanced manner.

Once you recognize that it is your responsibility to both succeed and safeguard society through a dynamic relationship of mutual care, you will take the necessary measures and actions to enhance both your own well-being and that of society. Practicing personal responsibility means caring for your health, community, family, and environment. This commitment fosters social responsibility, making you a valuable member of society. Indeed, the world would be better if personal responsibility were central to everyone's actions and interactions.

Pillars of Personal Responsibility

Attempting to define all the components of personal responsibility can be daunting. However, I would like to specify some elements that I think are particularly important in building personal responsibility in our lives. I have listed eight components: self-discipline, integrity, ethical behavior, accountability, altruism, perseverance, Continuous self-improvement, and diligence.

1. *Self-Discipline*

Self-discipline is a crucial element of personal responsibility. It involves setting priorities and living by them. More than just a trait, self-discipline empowers you to regulate your resources effectively based on established priorities.

Merriam-Webster defines self-discipline as the "correction or regulation of oneself for the sake of improvement."[6] The terms "correction" and "regulation" resonate deeply. They suggest that with self-discipline, you become your own regulator, prepared to adjust your actions as necessary to achieve your goals. This autonomy implies that no external

---

[6] Merriam-Webster, s.v. "Self-discipline," accessed April 16, 2024, https://www.merriam-webster.com/dictionary/self-discipline.

force is needed to compel you to do what is right; your decisions are self-motivated and self-directed.

You effectively become your own boss, recognizing that wisely managing resources, including time and money, is the responsible path. The importance of self-discipline spans various fields, including sports, where it is non-negotiable. Consider the Most Valuable Player (MVP) in sports like basketball, football, or baseball. Achieving MVP status requires rigorous self-discipline. Training schedules are non-negotiable because they are crucial for success. Self-discipline, in practice, demonstrates your commitment to your personal goals. I recall those nights when I stayed up until dawn, reviewing materials before final exams to ensure that my goal of being at the top of the class was met. An individual with self-discipline takes responsibility for their personal aspirations and priorities. Moreover, self-discipline means that others benefit from your behavior because they do not need to spend time disciplining you or completing your assigned tasks. I tip my hat to my two children, who demonstrated remarkable self-discipline during their upbringing. Their mother and I did not have to oversee their schoolwork. They understood that their responsibility was to complete their daily homework and prepare for their exams. Indeed, self-discipline benefits the individual who exhibits it and everyone they interact with. It is essential for outstanding individual achievement and collective performance.

2. *Integrity*

Integrity is an essential building block of personal responsibility. It embodies a personal commitment to upholding ethical principles and standards. Integrity encompasses honesty and sincerity—qualities that ensure we never lose the trust of our partners. This is a hallmark of personal responsibility because lost trust often leads to broken relationships. Those deemed untrustworthy may find themselves excluded from future business opportunities.

Maintaining honesty is challenging. Our society has many corrupt individuals at every level who will go to great lengths to compromise your honesty, sincerity, and adherence to ethical norms. It is vital to adhere strictly to standards of integrity and resist the temptations of money, positions, or other opportunities. For instance, I recall former bank tellers in Haiti who faced offers of bribes intended to make them violate their banks' rules. Thanks to their parents' values of integrity, they resisted these bribes, understanding that no amount of money could replace their family's reputation. Conversely, those tellers who succumbed to corruption were compelled to flee the country due to legal repercussions, consequently suffering the loss of their professional reputation and enduring considerable damage to their careers.

Similarly, in America, numerous local, state, and national officials have faced prosecution for integrity violations in America. Seeing council members, representatives, or senators lose their positions due to ethical failings is disheartening. Such cases can devastate the country, as some professionals represent invaluable assets. It is critical to understand that American public officials face severe consequences if they accept bribes, even minor ones, such as a free lunch while serving in their official capacities. Honesty benefits everyone and creates a trustworthy government that can effectively serve the public interest. This illustrates why integrity is such an integral part of personal responsibility.

Those who prioritize honesty believe that principles hold more value than monetary gain. They live by the sacred rule of the English proverb: "A good name is better than riches." Reflecting on this, I often share a valuable lesson from one of my loyal customers: "Always remember that a good reputation is like smoke; once it dissipates, it can never be restored."

3. *Ethical Behavior*

Ethical behavior involves actions guided by a set of moral values, helping us discern right from wrong and compelling us to choose the correct path conscientiously. Merriam-Webster defines ethics as "the discipline dealing with what is good and bad;

and with moral duty and obligation."[7] These concepts of moral duty and obligation lead us directly into personal responsibility. Personal responsibility compels us to act within moral duty and obligation boundaries. We do not simply make decisions. We also evaluate them based on what our conscience tells us unless we act solely for outcomes, disregarding what our conscience dictates. Although moral values may not mean the same thing to everyone, the human conscience has the capacity to question a person's actions to determine their righteousness. In many academic curricula, including business degrees, a class on ethics is commonly incorporated. This inclusion reflects the recognition that professionals, whether they are business leaders, engineers, healthcare providers, or public administrators, will encounter situations that demand ethical behavior. Ethical behavior is vital because our public and private leaders can harm our society if they act without conscience and moral duty. It serves as a moral compass for everyone who understands that actions have consequences. Humans must uphold specific values as guiding principles for behavior and decisions.

---

[7] Ethics," s.v., Merriam-Webster, accessed [April 19,2024. https://www.merriam-webster.com/dictionary/ethics.

4. Accountability

Accountability is a crucial aspect of personal responsibility, essential for individuals at all levels of any organization or society. It involves taking ownership of one's actions and their consequences. With accountability comes the commitment to consistently produce effective results, which one can proudly own and be prepared to accept the consequences. Merriam-Webster defines accountability as "an obligation or willingness to accept responsibility or to account for one's actions."[8]

For example, if you are an engineer and secure a contract to build a house with your construction team, the homeowner and society expect you to be accountable for the building's durability and safety. This expectation applies universally whenever a task is assigned, particularly within an organizational context. You must ensure everything is done correctly because you are ultimately responsible for your actions, results, and consequences.

Accountable individuals are invaluable assets because they care deeply about the outcomes of their work and strive to complete tasks successfully. Such professionals often work

---

[8] Merriam-Webster, s.v. "Accountability," accessed April 17, 2024, https://www.merriam-webster.com/dictionary/accountability.

beyond required hours because they believe that once a task is assigned, its completion is a sacred duty. They will do everything they can to finish their assigned tasks and responsibilities on time and with a high degree of excellence. No salary can truly compensate for the value of a genuinely accountable professional.

When you fully own your actions, decisions, and consequences, you become an asset to your organization, family, and society. Accountability remains a fundamental component of personal responsibility.

5. *Altruism*

I have identified altruism as a critical component of personal responsibility due to the direct link between our individual well-being and the stability of our community. Merriam-Webster defines altruism as "unselfish regard for or devotion to the welfare of others."[9] This definition underscores the connection between altruism and personal responsibility, positioning altruism as the act or habit of caring for others. When we care for our neighbor's children, for example, we contribute to the safety of our neighborhood and protect our peace. Caring for others transcends spiritual or religious obligations; it is about recognizing that

---

[9] Merriam-Webster, s.v. "Altruism," accessed April 17, 2024, https://www.merriam-webster.com/dictionary/altruism

our stability is deeply intertwined with the well-being of our community and society.

For instance, ensuring that every child attends school will build a society with fewer reports of delinquency and violence. Recently, I encountered a social media argument suggesting seniors should not pay taxes for public schools because they do not have school-age children. In response, I argued that while seniors may not have children in school, the education of young people benefits everyone. Without education, children may face challenges that can lead to societal issues affecting seniors and other community members. Our tax contributions are not just transactions tied directly to our personal needs; they are investments in societal stability, ensuring the welfare of every community member.

Social justice, equity, and fairness are integral to this concept of personal responsibility. Being personally responsible essentially involves practicing love without religious connotations. By caring for others, we also care for ourselves, making altruism not just a moral choice but a pragmatic one. This doesn't mean giving away everything we own; instead, it means recognizing ourselves as part of a larger society where the challenges others face can indirectly impact our stability.

Economic studies recommend ensuring equity or protection for the majority because if the people's basic needs are not satisfied, revolutions could occur, thus destabilizing the whole economy. Therefore, taking care of others is not just an ethical requirement but a necessity for both social and economic stability. When you act altruistically in your decisions and actions, you not only contribute to the greater good but also indirectly enhance your own well-being. Altruistic behavior reinforces personal responsibility.

6. *Perseverance*

Perseverance is a concept that resonates deeply because it is intrinsically linked to personal responsibility. Why is perseverance such a crucial aspect of personal responsibility? It entails a steadfast commitment to one's tasks and goals. Without a firm commitment, a goal is meaningless. Many people abandon their projects prematurely as if they intend to flip from one initiative to another without taking anything to completion. Merriam-Webster defines perseverance as "continued effort to do or achieve something despite difficulties, failure, or opposition."[10] Indeed, perseverance exemplifies the tenacity of individuals who pursue their aspirations and goals, no matter the obstacles.

---

[10] Merriam-Webster, s.v. "Perseverance," accessed April 17, 2024, https://www.merriam-webster.com/dictionary/perseverance.

This internal fortitude empowers one to become even more resilient in the face of adversity. Challenges, failures, and setbacks do not deter the resilient; instead, they fuel their determination to strive for the finish line.

My dad provided me with a profound example of perseverance during my childhood. As a diligent parent, he displayed remarkable resilience when my youngest sister, Elsie, then only a year old, fell critically ill with typhoid fever and nearly lost her life at the State University Hospital in Port-au-Prince, Haiti, also known as the general hospital. He held some doubts about the hospital's capability to save her life. Therefore, determined not to give up on her, he asked that they release the baby. The hospital hesitated to release her; then, he used his connections with Haiti's Minister of Health to ensure she was discharged. When he brought her home, he administered a medicine that an outpatient clinic prescribed. He was told by the prescribing doctor that the medicine could aid her recovery. Following the administration of the drug, Elsie began to recover. However, the ordeal was not without its hardships. Taking care of the baby at home required a lot of adjustments, and my dad could not really go to work. I vividly recall Elsie's pain-filled cries, "Abè glas," pleading with my dad, Robert, for ice to ease her discomfort. In the summer of 1979, my dad's unwavering perseverance overcame the illness, and his efforts were subsequently rewarded with an opportunity to relocate to the United States, providing a better future for his six children. My dad emerged victorious from this arduous battle solely through his resilience and unwavering faith in God, exemplifying his deep commitment to his paternal duties and to preserving his daughter's well-being.

The spirit of perseverance is also vividly illustrated in American professional sports, particularly in the best-of-seven series format found in basketball, baseball, and hockey. These series allow athletes to demonstrate resilience and resolve before the public eye. I am continually impressed by teams that overcome substantial deficits, rallying with tremendous strength and moral fortitude to triumph. American sports offer a vivid illustration of resilience, with players demonstrating immense responsibility through their perseverance and determination to secure a championship. They strive for success but must also cultivate a deep sense of personal responsibility, contributing to their team's success through resilience and positivity.

I exhort you to never surrender in the face of difficulties. Demonstrate persistence daily as you navigate obstacles in your quest for success and outstanding performance. Your perseverance displays your commitment to your responsibilities and transforms setbacks into remarkable comebacks, ultimately granting you the sweet taste of success.

7. Continuous Self-Improvement

Continuous self-improvement is straightforward—it entails a relentless pursuit of better methods in the daily activities of your professional and personal life. This pursuit is key to excellence and is essential for personal responsibility as it demonstrates a profound commitment to enhancing your outcomes. A dedication to continuous improvement ensures you remain at the peak of your game.

This aspect of personal responsibility is critical in contexts such as American professional sports. Continuous self-improvement is among the most crucial attributes of a Most Valuable Player (MVP). To be the best or among the top in your field, relentless self-enhancement is indispensable. It requires the acquisition of new skills and the refinement of existing ones. As a professional or entrepreneur, you must continuously learn new techniques and stay abreast of the latest discoveries, theories, and methods, ensuring exceptional performance in the marketplace.

Never cease learning; the quest for knowledge never ends if you aim to excel in your industry or achieve outstanding results. Continuous self-improvement paves the way to success in the marketplace. My high school philosophy teacher, Mr. Jabouin, once remarked, "There are qualities you possess that compel decision-makers to take notice; they simply cannot ignore you." By embracing personal responsibility and integrating continuous self-improvement into your personal and professional life, success is not just probable—it is almost assured because the marketplace cannot afford to overlook someone who is constantly advancing and improving.

Ultimately, the quality of your work will always benefit your organization and society, making you a priceless asset.

8. *Diligence*

I have identified diligence as an additional cornerstone of personal responsibility. It is prominently featured on the components list because when individuals understand their role in effecting change, they do not procrastinate. Instead, they invest steady, earnest, and energetic effort in their tasks. Merriam-Webster defines diligence as "steady, earnest, and energetic effort: devoted and painstaking work and application to accomplish an undertaking."[11] This definition highlights the importance of diligence in actively pursuing and achieving desired goals without delay.

Once you are convinced that an action is the right thing to do, do not delay. Allocate time for the task at hand.

---

[11] Merriam-Webster, s.v. "Diligence," accessed April 17, 2024, https://www.merriam-webster.com/dictionary/diligence.

The future is uncertain; what you do now becomes a lasting asset. Tomorrow is never guaranteed. You probably know people who constantly plan to return to school or learn a new skill, understanding that it could transform their professional and financial situations. Yet, they keep postponing these plans until they abandon them altogether. Act now if you are convinced it is the right and responsible thing to do.

Viktor Frankl and the Statue of Personal Responsibility Project

I never realized I was following in the footsteps of Viktor Frankl until I embarked on my book project about success. Surprisingly, given my academic background in business, focusing on finance, marketing, and leadership, I was unaware of his name. Frankl is an Austrian psychiatrist and Holocaust survivor who founded the discipline of logotherapy. In chapter 4, which focuses on personal life's mission, we will delve deeper into logotherapy and explore some concepts found in Frankl's writings and legacy.

To me, being a disciple means embodying the teachings of the expert, which catalyzes our inherent knowledge to the surface. I aim to provide a solution for everyone, especially the newer generations, who often get lost in artificial definitions of success. I am convinced that these misguided pursuits can lead to severe mental health issues.

I consider myself a natural disciple of Viktor Frankl because I carry many of the ideas he explained in his logotherapy theory, encompassing therapy through meaning. Frankl's teachings have confirmed my thoughts about the dire consequences of a lack of meaning, ultimately expressed in a life mission, even though I only became aware of logotherapy by exploring the Japanese concept of ikigai. Through this work, I hope to provide a more meaningful path to success that fosters well-being and genuine fulfillment.

Viktor Frankl's works help support the point I intend to make. Even though his objectives aim to heal mental health patients, he helps us understand the importance of finding our life's meaning, which is another way to figure out our mission. I am profoundly grateful to him for laying a solid foundation for my writing outcomes. By embracing the value of meaning in our lives and maintaining personal responsibility, we equip ourselves to confront life's challenges with realism and pragmatism, thereby uncovering the positive aspects of our experiences.

In my search for answers, I have found him to be a guiding light for today's youth. His teachings on life's meaning and the importance of personal responsibility serve as invaluable lessons for everyone.

Viktor Frankl proposed erecting a "Statue of Responsibility" on the West Coast of America, mirroring the iconic Statue of Liberty on the East Coast. According to Frankl, freedom and personal responsibility are inseparable; they form an oxymoron, as both concepts are intertwined. One cannot fully grasp freedom without acknowledging the importance of personal responsibility, as it upholds and maintains individual freedoms.

I strongly support the proposed project he inspired because I am deeply disturbed by the sight of people of all ages fighting for their freedom with total disregard for their personal responsibility. This was painfully evident during the COVID-19 crisis in America, where many advocated that their individual freedom entitled them to not wear masks, despite the large numbers of people dying in hospitals throughout the country. I could never understand this advocacy for freedom without a solid link to responsibility.

Viktor Frankl's vision is sustained through ongoing efforts to build the Statue of Responsibility. A dedicated foundation exists for this noble project, and I made a donation to the foundation to demonstrate my genuine support for promoting personal responsibility in America. I encourage you to visit statueofresponsibility.org for more information on this initiative inspired by Dr. Frankl.

I have witnessed the consequences of a lack of personal responsibility throughout my life, especially growing up in Haiti, where single mothers raise many children without support from their fathers. Unlike in America, where the legal system enforces child support rigorously, Haiti's legal framework offers little support to these mothers. This situation is truly outrageous. Surprisingly, one father confessed to me that he targeted women with entrepreneurial skills, giving them a small sum of money to free himself from further parental responsibilities.

My moral outrage deepens when I contemplate that while many politicians misappropriate funds from the public treasury, millions of children in Haiti endure deprivation of food, education, and healthcare, with most of the population lacking access to essential services. I hold that those who embezzle public funds are even more reprehensible than kidnappers or gang members, as their actions indirectly lead to the deaths of thousands of children every day.

If these politicians practiced personal responsibility, Haiti could thrive. Perhaps, inspired by Dr. Frankl's proposal, I should advocate for a similar "Statue of Responsibility" project in Haiti. On a larger scale, when the majority embraces personal responsibility, it holds the power to resolve numerous national and global challenges.

Corruption is a global epidemic, with government officials accepting bribes on procurements, leading to inflated costs that taxpayers ultimately pay. This represents a profound lack of personal responsibility among leaders who are duty-bound to protect the citizens of their countries, particularly the most vulnerable. Additionally, in the business world, we talk about corporate social responsibility (CSR), which requires companies to ensure that their decisions are socially responsible and do not harm society. If business leaders and public servants exercise personal responsibility, our society will greatly benefit from enhanced economic and social stability. In contrast, if individuals are solely committed to protecting their freedom without regard for responsibility, they can destroy a country's fabric.

To conclude this chapter, I reflect on a statement by Adam Sicinski, who has written about the four pillars of personal responsibility. He states: "The four pillars of responsibility include being responsible for our aims and goals in life; for what we focus on and give our attention to; for our attitude; and for our actions." He also remarks, "When we take full responsibility for these four areas of our lives, that is when the magic happens. That's when life takes on new meaning, and this subsequently helps us work with a higher level of intentional purpose toward the accomplishment of our most important and meaningful goals."

Today, I humbly invite you to integrate the principles of personal responsibility into your life. By embracing personal responsibility, you will not only enhance your chances of personal success but also contribute to creating a better society. In the next chapter, we will explore the MVP-PA success model, which offers further insights into achieving success with meaning.

Chapter 3
The MVP-PA Model and The Culture of Success

A Framework for Achieving Your Goals

"Being busy does not always mean real work. The object of all work is production or accomplishment and to either of these ends there must be forethought, system, planning, intelligence, and honest purpose, as well as perspiration. Seeming to do is not doing."[12]

– Thomas A. Edison

Many books on success delve into the habits, characteristics, and personal anecdotes of extraordinarily successful individuals. While these titles abound, it is uncommon to encounter a book that conceptualizes success as a systematic process, delineating a series of clear, actionable steps designed

---

[12] Thomas A. Edison Quotes. BrainyQuote.com. Accessed December 18, 2023. https://www.brainyquote.com/quotes/thomas_a_edison_131294.

to reliably guide one toward achievement. Recognizing that success stems from such systematic approaches ensures consistent achievement across various projects. In the realms of management and administration, project management remains a vital tool for organizations. Similarly, applying project management principles to personal endeavors makes success a more realistic and attainable goal.

3The MVP-PA Success Model

I have developed the MVP-PA model, as seen in Figure 3, to facilitate personal success. This straightforward yet effective system is tailored for individual success and simplifies the resolution process by dissecting and understanding each problem component. A simple system like the MVP-PA model proves invaluable in a world where complexities often overwhelm our lives. Comprising five steps—Mission, Vision, Passion, Plan, and Action—this model not only helps you achieve your goals but also aids the world in accomplishing more, thereby improving people's lives and meeting your life's expectations.

With the MVP-PA model, you will consistently grasp the big picture and expertly manage the complexities of any challenge. Successful people have a habit of simplifying their problems, and through the MVP-PA model, we aim to build this habit.

The MVP-PA Model: Your Personal Life as a Project

Presenting a clear roadmap to success remains my priority. You need to know what to do when solving a problem. The approach for success represented in the MVP-PA model asks you to treat your life as a project or a set of multiple sub-projects. Viewing your life as a project requires a clear understanding of your challenges. This is what is referred to as problem identification. Your life is viewed as a complex problem to solve. After identifying and dissecting your life's challenges, you can brainstorm potential solutions and set a clear objective. That general objective can be considered your vision statement. The vision statement plays a vital role in the success model because this is when you define the ideal scope of the expected or aspired accomplishments. Once you set yourself an unobstructed vision, you need to justify the project of your life. If you were to present a project to a donor, you would need to answer why you think the project deserves to be funded. In project management, this would be viewed as the project justification. This is the passion stage in our model. You are the one justifying your mission to yourself. You are your own donor. You must answer a simple question: Why is your life project important to you? You do not need to proceed if you cannot justify the project to yourself. This may not be your real mission if you are not convinced about the project's validity and feasibility. When your mission can be justified, you will build a plan with a specific and clear goal for what you aspire to accomplish to make your vision a reality. You can define a roadmap to turn your vision into reality, but that plan is worthless without concrete actions to execute it. This becomes the core of your life mission or project. Follow these steps to be successful in your life, and whenever you face a challenging situation or crisis, you can use the same model to transform setbacks into victories.

However, defining the elements of a successful life or career is essential. The following is a list of components or factors that will propel you to success. Some people will have all of them, some will have a few, and some will make it simply because one component is so dominant that it helps them reach the apex of their career.

Factors of Success

1. Sense of Direction

If I were to encounter you in the streets and ask, "What are you doing now, or what is your plan?" I would expect you to be short, specific, and clear about what you intend to do. Some people cannot articulate where they are going with their life or their current life project in two minutes. In sales, we talk about the elevator pitch or speech[13]. An elevator pitch is a brief, persuasive speech that aims to sell an organization, product, or service in less than two minutes. Similarly, you should be able to explain your life project in two minutes or less succinctly. You need to have an unclouded vision of your destination, current or future. That is why the MVP-PA model remains so significant. The model forces every individual to have a clear goal and focus on a valid plan for their life. You cannot accomplish durable success if you have no real focus on one specific project or goal. You should know the distance to run to reach the finish line and focus on the destination. Knowing your finish line lets you determine when and how to reach it. This allows you to measure your progress in terms of time and accomplishments.

---

[13] Harvard FAS Mignone Center for Career Success. "How to Create an Elevator Pitch (With Examples)." Accessed June 11, 2024. https://careerservices.fas.harvard.edu/blog/2022/10/11/how-to-create-an-elevator-pitch-with-examples/.

2. *Optimism*

People will have a tough time succeeding if they approach their life projects with pessimism. They need to be convinced that they can achieve success and greatness. If they believe that the sun will never rise for them, they may force their sun not to rise by blocking the sunshine with negative expectations. Winners are those who are convinced that they deserve victory like everyone else and that success can smile upon them. Great projects demand optimism. You need to see hope. When you are an optimist, you grab failures by the horns and become resilient, confident in your ability to turn them into victories. Your obstacles cannot stop you; instead, they give you more stamina to work harder and find more effective and creative solutions. While others focus on threats, a true optimist and practitioner of success sees opportunities.

3. *Service*

The service factor refers to a person's ability to be humble and offer excellent service to their customers or stakeholders. If someone does not provide good customer service, they will experience hardship as professionals or entrepreneurs. Customers are willing to pay extra for good service. If you are humble, listen to your customers or stakeholders, and are willing to go the extra mile to satisfy them, your success is almost guaranteed, provided you have the right product and a positive attitude.

4. *Continuous Learning*

In today's dynamic professional landscape, the willingness to embrace new knowledge and innovative concepts is essential for maintaining competitiveness and expertise in any field. Expanding your knowledge base enhances your effectiveness as a professional or entrepreneur, enabling you to navigate complex challenges proficiently. Moreover, cultivating transferable skills—such as verbal and nonverbal communication, active listening, and proficient writing—equips you to excel across various roles. Familiarity with modern computer skills further enhances your capabilities, providing a distinct competitive edge.

Historically, reading was the primary pathway to acquiring knowledge essential for ongoing personal and professional development. However, the contemporary world offers unprecedented resources, including search engines, educational websites, and advanced AI-driven teaching tools, which previous generations lacked. In this era of abundant information and accessible learning tools, the failure to continually advance one's knowledge base is inexcusable. Continuous learning is essential and offers a profound opportunity to thrive in an ever-evolving world.

5. *Prioritizing Long-Term Success*

Success sometimes requires making quick decisions to respond to market conditions. However, your life mission will require you to prioritize the long-term over the short-term. When you work, aim to secure day-to-day success while also building long-term success. You do not want to have a nice check today and lose all your customers in two years. You must plan for durability, and this is one characteristic of those looking for *success with meaning*. Your strategies and tactics as a professional or an entrepreneur should never be short-sighted. The short-term view looks at outcomes, and the long-term view looks at the process. If you think of your life as a result that stops in time, it is easy to get discouraged that you have failed. However, if you view your life as a work in progress and commit to improving it daily, you will become stronger and stronger until you achieve sustainable success.

6. *Networking*

Networking is a critical success factor, opening doors to opportunities through valuable connections. You can become successful simply because you are in touch with successful people in society. Those successful people can help you in your journey of success because they can guide you in the direction they have explored during previous experiences. I can attest that I have had many life opportunities because I networked with people who could help me advance professionally. I succeeded in some areas because I sought help when needed. This was one of the components that helped me secure a scholarship to study in America. By networking with successful professionals, I was well-equipped to seize the opportunity. Maintain a network of professionals who can help you move upward on the success ladder. You will be able to get what you need to succeed, whether professionally or as an entrepreneur.

7. *Adaptability*

Adaptability can be defined as your capacity to adjust yourself to new circumstances and environments. Complex business environments and market changes will compel individuals and organizations to alter their habits and ways of doing things. Your ability to adapt to changes is vital for success in your journey of achievement. The new world demands adaptability as technology advances, altering every aspect of our lives. You must be prepared to learn new software your company plans to implement, whether next month or year. It is commonly said that, in some organizations, change is constant. This holds particularly true today, as organizations that fail to adapt will be surpassed by their competitors. Successful people typically possess the ability to adapt to new environments or understand they have no choice but to adapt. If you aspire to succeed, you must follow them and embrace adaptability.

8. *Persistence*

Anyone who watches the NBA or any professional sport understands what persistence entails. It's the ability to confront challenges and setbacks with determination and resilience while confident that your efforts will transform deficits into ultimate victories. Sustainable success demands such persistence. Stay strong and never stop fighting to bring your mission to fruition. I tip my hat to the many friends and family members who tirelessly strive for success and the young professionals who return to school amid economic downturns or constant layoffs in their primary industries. Without a doubt, persistence is an essential ingredient for personal achievement.

9. *Emotional Intelligence*

I recall a conversation with one of my coworkers where he mentioned emotional intelligence as one of his brother's strengths. He acknowledged that he may not be considered the most intelligent man, but he has succeeded because of his emotional intelligence. During our discussion, we concluded that emotional intelligence often proves more crucial than raw intellect in the quest for success. Merriam-Webster defines emotional intelligence as "the ability to recognize, understand, and deal skillfully with one's own emotions and the emotions of others" (as by regulating one's emotions or by showing empathy and good judgment in social interactions).' This is precisely what my friend was referring to. When you can skillfully navigate your emotions and those of others, you can build effective relationships, paving the way for personal and business success. I believe many CEOs have reached the pinnacle of success not solely because of their intellectual intelligence but because of their emotional intelligence. As they are among the professionals earning the highest rewards, it is clear that emotional intelligence is a vital ingredient in the recipe for outstanding achievement.

10. *Financial Education*

Many people face significant challenges in life simply because they lack a basic education in financial management principles. I believe that education in schools should focus more on the practical aspects of daily living. When people are trained in the everyday necessities of life, they can better manage daily issues and solve their problems. This understanding is crucial, as demonstrated in my next point about the importance of savings.

While working in the mortgage industry, I learned that consistent saving is essential for financial strength. Entering excessive debt can obstruct the path to financial stability. It is a fundamental rule to save at least 10% of one's income to build financial security. Yet, it is common for individuals to open various lines of credit, often spending more than they can afford. Young adults should understand that credit should primarily be used for investments rather than consumption. For instance, when purchasing a car, consider it an investment in your professional life; select a vehicle with manageable payments. Prioritize functionality over luxury. Likewise, buying a home should be seen as an investment. Over time, you will build equity—your own capital in the house—which can be a significant financial resource or collateral. Borrowing to secure your job or business should also be considered an investment in your professional or entrepreneurial growth.

Are you familiar with the saying "cash is king"? This phrase means that having cash puts you in a strong position because it allows you to seize opportunities. Liquidity refers to the ability of an asset to be quickly converted into cash; by definition, cash is the most liquid asset. As an economic actor, meeting all your monthly obligations on time is crucial, so having available cash is necessary. Before pursuing an opportunity, it is wise to ask yourself if you can still meet your monthly obligations after investing in this opportunity. You need to maintain liquid assets to protect your long-term investments. A liquidity crisis can severely damage your financial stability, including affecting your credit score, a crucial element of your financial health in America. Liquidity crises can even cause bankruptcy. The country learned the value of liquidity in financial stability when the real estate market crashed in 2008. Understanding that these principles apply to personal finance and business management is vital.

Finance is a crucial part of our lives. Everyone needs to know how to manage a monthly budget. With basic financial knowledge, people can recognize when to apply for a loan before it's too late. For instance, if you know that there may be layoffs at your company and you own a house with equity, it might be wise to apply for a home equity line of credit before losing your job, as securing a loan can be more challenging once unemployed. Additionally, foundational knowledge in finance is instrumental when venturing into business, as my experience shows.

Basic financial education also enables you to start a small business with less stress because you understand how to present to the bank what you need in terms of financing based on your initial owner's investment. The Small Business Administration offers training seminars on small business management that are highly beneficial for aspiring entrepreneurs. In 1994, I participated in one such seminar in Seattle, Washington, while completing my small business management class at Edmonds Community College. The experience was incredibly instructive, underscoring the importance of educating oneself in fundamental financial principles to achieve business success.

11. Health and Well-being

No health, no success—it is that simple. In my culture, on New Year's Day, people often wish each other good health because they believe you can achieve everything else with good health. When I speak of good health, I mean both physical and mental, as both are crucial for balance, longevity, endurance, and happiness.

In my line of work, I have encountered many individuals who had to halt their professional or entrepreneurial endeavors due to health issues. These issues can range from physical stamina limitations to mental health challenges. For example, after many years of employment and a willingness to continue working, one lady was compelled to inform her employer that she could no longer work because her memory was failing. This is a poignant reminder that your health maintains your wealth and success.

Taking care of your health is essential to achieving outstanding success. There is a direct correlation between health, wealth, and personal achievement. Prioritizing your health is necessary to succeed and fulfill your mission.

In your journey towards success, emphasize your focus on your specific mission or goal. It is crucial not to compare your life to others' results, as your environment, goals, plans, vision, and projects are unique. Understanding success factors enables you to adjust for better performance in your personal and professional endeavors. Your life is meant to offer an exceptional contribution to the world.

Maintain a clear sense of direction, stay optimistic, and affirm your desired remarkable outcomes. Commit to delivering excellent customer service to your stakeholders. Stay open to learning and adapting with innovative ideas, strategies, and skills. Focus not only on short-term gains but also on building a sustainable life project. Your journey toward *success with meaning* is an ongoing process that upholds your MVP status.

The MVP-PA Model: The Path to an MVP Status

The MVP-PA model is naturally related to the MVP (Most Valuable Player) title used in American professional sports. In the NBA, 'MVP' stands for Most Valuable Player. The MVP-PA model redefines this acronym to form the foundation for becoming the most valuable player in your discipline. Here is what MVP stands for in this context:

- **M stands for Mission**: The Most Valuable Player has a clearly defined mission. You should make it a priority to have a clear mission.
- **V stands for Vision**: The MVP possesses a vision that extends beyond being average, aiming to be the best or among the best players globally. You should have a clear set of aspirations to achieve greatness for your mission.
- **P stands for Passion**: The MVP harbors a passion for the game that transcends simple motivation, becoming an obsession and a lifestyle. They continually strive to improve, dedicating considerable time and resources toward their goal. Your passion represents the power of transformation within you. Passion makes champions.

Once you know what you want and where to go in life, you need a written action plan. This plan is essential in the journey to success. After designing this plan with the necessary steps, you must take action to execute it. This plan will help you identify and gather all the ingredients or resources needed to achieve your life project or mission. Action will be the vehicle of transformation for your specific aspirations.

My goal with this book is to enable every reader to become an MVP in their field and successfully accomplish their mission. Some readers may discover that they have already followed the steps outlined in the model without realizing it. Most successful people have clear goals about where they want to go, a clear aspiration for the scope of their realization, and a plan while they take action constantly to realize their visions. These natural MVPs should help those around them understand the MVP-PA concepts to achieve outstanding performance. The MVP-PA model will empower you to be one of the world's MVPs in your field.

Consider LeBron James. He is an MVP because:

- He understood his mission, continually striving to excel and innovate in basketball.
- He maintained a visionary outlook, aiming to become a global sports ambassador and influence basketball worldwide.
- He nurtured a deep passion for the game, driving his continuous improvement, commitment, and motivation.

LeBron's journey illustrates that success is not just about talent but also clear intent and dedication. You need to be determined to invest resources, including time, and work tirelessly if you want outstanding achievement. By clearly identifying your mission, defining a vision that surpasses ordinary goals, and developing a profound passion for your endeavors, you position yourself to become an MVP in life. A true MVP understands their Mission, Vision, and Passion intimately—they live and breathe their MVP. With that MVP

(Mission, Vision, Passion) mentality, a plan executed with purposeful actions will make the dream of becoming the *Most Valuable Player* a reality.

Think about how the world would be better if everyone took full responsibility for fulfilling their life's mission. If everyone embraced the belief that they have a unique role to fulfill, our world would transform into a place far greater than we can currently imagine. Humanity's potential achievements and advancements would be boundless and extraordinary under such a collective mindset. When individuals take their personal mission seriously, many opportunities and possibilities unfold.

Realizing that you are well-equipped to face the task at hand is a wonderful way to arm yourself to perform your mission successfully. The following section intends to convince you that your inner potential will give you what it takes to aim for an MPV status.

You Are Worth More Than You Think

The day of your enlightenment will come when you realize that the world's perfection depends on you. Think of your life as the unique color an artist needs to complete their masterpiece—the painting of humanity. Inside of you, a small voice must recognize how indispensable you are to the world. Like every human being, you have an irreplaceable contribution to make.

Your freedom will be realized when you accept that the world owes you nothing. Miserable are those who believe someone else owes them something and take pleasure in blaming others for their failures. You will never achieve extraordinary success until you choose to give rather than receive, to initiate rather than wait, to contribute rather than expect contributions, and to take the first step instead of siding with those who fear being laughed at. Giving is powerful. You are well-equipped as an individual. Today is the day to take stock of your countless resources.

Sometimes, you may feel less valuable than you truly are. Underestimating your worth can lead to a sense of having little to offer. The subconscious mind is immensely powerful, governing your actions and reactions. Therefore, reprogramming your subconscious is fundamental.

WYSIWYG (What You See Is What You Get) is an old acronym taught to computer users and students. I propose a new acronym for the subconscious mind: WYPIWYG (What You Plant Is What You Get). This means that what you cultivate in your subconscious will manifest in your life. You must use your words, thoughts, and actions skillfully as they combine to create the results of your life. You are what you think. However, the challenge with the subconscious mind is that you are not the only one programming it. Unless you have mastered the law of attraction and can block negative influences from social media, TV shows, news, and people around you, your subconscious is susceptible to these external inputs that affect you unconsciously.

Always see yourself as one of the world's solutions, a problem-solver, a deliverer—just as my dad saw himself for his home village. Sometimes, you may think being a deliverer means you need to do extraordinary things. However, that is not always necessary. A simple smile daily to someone who needs it can mean the world. Being a problem solver doesn't mean you have to solve major world problems. Sometimes, it means being the go-to person at your job or motivating a neighborhood adolescent.

I invite you to use your immeasurable potential to make a difference in people's lives. As an infinite power source, you can contribute to humanity's evolution. You must believe that you can, as we will explore in the next section.

Believe in Yourself

It is time to silence that negative inner voice. Your capacity goes beyond measure. Listen to the little voice telling you that you can soar. Nobody can gauge your ability to achieve—only your beliefs and attitude can impede your growth. I urge you to catch the achievement vibe, surround yourself with people who can boost your self-esteem, and push you to the limits of your accomplishments. The people you interact with can help reinforce the positive inner voice that enables you to believe in yourself. Whenever someone says, "You can," they help build the confidence you need to move forward. However, if I were to say that you only need to believe in yourself, I would be underestimating the powerful influence of your environment. When someone has a group of friends constantly encouraging them, we expect that individual to progress.

On the contrary, being surrounded by negativity can hinder your growth. Nonetheless, you must take responsibility. Whenever my friends say I cannot achieve something, it fuels my drive to prove them wrong. You need to develop a protective shield against negative influences. When people say you cannot do something, counteract their negativity with your words and thoughts. Every "you cannot" should be immediately substituted with a powerful "I CAN." You have the ultimate control over shaping your destiny for success. Do not place blame elsewhere. For instance, the leader of General Motors cannot attribute the company's failures solely to employees or competitors. Apart from uncontrollable events like the COVID-19 crisis, the future of any organization—and, similarly, your results—rests on its leadership. You must always take full responsibility. You must believe in yourself and make things happen, enabling you to shine as you were meant to.

You are responsible, not others. Acknowledging your responsibility plays a key role in shaping your success. Once you realize you are accountable, you seek solutions to all your challenges. Blaming others sends a message to your subconscious mind that you don't need to worry about it because someone else is in charge. You should take ownership of every aspect of your life. This is the only way you will rise above challenges, just as an eagle uses the storm to soar to greater heights. The eagle does not let the wind diminish its potential but instead uses it to fly higher and leverage the opportunities presented by the storm. By thinking like an eagle, you assume control over your problems and use every situation to improve your life and enhance your results.

Joan of Arc's story compels us to respond to our life's calling with bravery and resilience, taking responsibility and rising to the occasion.

Joan of Arc: A Timeless Tale of Mission and Courage

The story of Joan of Arc remains a profound source of inspiration, even centuries after her heroic deeds. At just thirteen years old, Joan was reportedly guided by a mysterious voice urging her to save France from English domination. By the age of seventeen, she had embraced this daunting mission and led the French army to significant victories despite her lack of formal training in leadership or combat.

Joan's dedication to her mission transformed her from a simple peasant girl into a pivotal figure in French history. Her unwavering belief and commitment inspired her soldiers and led to several victories. Beyond the battlefield, her dedication also brought tangible benefits to her community; her efforts were rewarded by the king with a decree that exempted her village, Domrémy, from taxes for about three hundred years.

Joan's story is not just about historical achievement; it reminds us of the power of listening to that inner voice that calls us to a greater purpose. Her life challenges us to consider: What mission is your inner voice urging you to undertake? How might your dedication to this mission change your life and the world that hosts you?

Embrace the call to action that resonates within you, as Joan did, and you may find that your mission can lead to achievements beyond your wildest expectations. However, there may be times when you do not feel any internal calling. In such cases, it is your responsibility to choose one mission from the many that the world presents. There will always be a need to satisfy, a problem to solve. Your role as a human being is to take responsibility for at least one of these problems.

My goal is to urge people to focus solely on one mission because dividing your attention among multiple missions impedes the full realization of the primary mission. You can engage in many activities but must laser-focus on one mission. That means all activities must contribute towards realizing your primary and unique mission.

I focus on success with meaning because the true worth of human lives emerges when we create something beyond fulfilling basic necessities. Animals satisfy their necessities in their own ways, as I have learned from my own dog, Alvin. We are the only beings on Earth capable of transforming the planet's reality through our actions. The provocative question for everyone is: What is your mission?

Joan of Arc's story shows us that your spot is unique. Nobody can fill it for you or perform a job better than you are capable of. Everyone has a spot specifically assigned to their name. No one else can take care of that spot uniquely assigned to us, no matter how smart or strong they are.

Occasionally, your inner voice will be like an angel's voice begging you to do something about a problem facing the world. If you ever feel that burning desire to intervene and do something, do not resist. The world must need your magical power, which you are unaware of, just like Joan of Arc did not know she could bring victory to France and restore the dignity of the French kingdom.

You have a mission, but the world is the one that will profit from its achievement. Never take your mission lightly. I recently lost a friend from high school, Jerry, who was fifty-one. Everyone who knew him was heartbroken by his passing. We are devastated by his death, as he was like a brother to us. Once again, I realize that we all have a mission to fulfill. Despite being the younger brother of one of our classmates, he managed to forge connections with most of the alumni from the 1989 class of College Canado-Haitien High School in Port-au-Prince, Haiti, making him the strongest and most genuine link among many of us. Isn't it true that we do not have an eternity?

His mission was clear: to bring love and comfort to the people around him by connecting with them through daily messages or meaningful pictures of the places he visited. He traveled the world, and wherever he went, he enjoyed sharing his experiences. Without knowing, Jerry was practicing the MVP-PA model. He had a mission he was passionate about and a vision of how he would show people affection through a structured plan of actions he executed daily with passion. His loving and caring personality exemplified the priceless value of his life and made him unforgettable. He fully lived his life's purpose.

In the next part of the book, we will individually address the Five Proven Steps of Life with Success found in the MVP-PA model: Mission, Vision, Passion, Plan, and Action. These stages will help you understand the concepts and prepare you to take action for a better life, actively contributing to building a better world while working on your personal success and a fulfilled life. We will challenge you to integrate these components into a mission-focused personal plan. This plan is designed to achieve success and propel your life toward profound fulfillment and significant achievements. Engage deeply, reflect on your personal goals, and prepare to discover your life mission and transform your approach to success.

Part II

The 5 Proven Steps to Life with Success

The MVP-PA Success Model

Chapter 4
Step 1: Define Your Mission

"Outstanding people have one thing in common: An absolute sense of mission."[14]

- Zig Ziglar

Finding your mission is crucial, as it is one of the most valuable steps in your life. It represents what endures even after we transition from this life or leave this world. Discovering your mission will propel your life to new heights, transforming it into an everlasting enterprise in the battle for a better world. My dad's life story is inspiring; he passed his mission to our family as a legacy for future generations. I rejoice, knowing that he did not truly die, as his life continues to manifest success through the continuity of his mission. I sincerely hope this chapter will inspire you to invest time and effort in finding your true life's mission, which is the foundation of your achievement and fulfillment.

---

[14] Zig Ziglar Quotes. BrainyQuote.com, Brainy Media Inc, 2023. https://www.brainyquote.com/quotes/zig_ziglar_617742, accessed December 18, 2023.

4Mission: Are You Making the World a Better Place?

My Dad's Mission

My dad originates from Haiti, and let me tell you, he has been my ultimate hero since I was just nine years old. He was my rock, inspiration source, and guide throughout his life. He instilled in me from an early age the value of family more than anything else. However, the most important lesson I learned from him remained the power of taking action to achieve personal and professional success. He was a champion of education and self-discipline. Even though he might not have fit the traditional mold of academic success, in my eyes, he surpassed the worth of many out there with fancy degrees.

He has contributed significantly to the success of many individuals in his family or his friends' families by advocating for education as a pathway to professional success. However, he did not leave school due to a lack of interest or capacity. He excelled academically and ranked among the top students in his elementary school classes. He left school in eighth grade out of necessity. Moving from his countryside hometown of Leogane to Port-au-Prince, Haiti's capital, he could not solely rely on his family's support to sustain himself. He had to find a way to produce income to support a more demanding life in the capital city of Haiti.

I was ten years old when he left Haiti in 1979. Before departing, he promised to fund one of his nephews his four-year college education to become a civil engineer—a promise he fulfilled. This commitment added to the burden of caring for seven children and two mothers. Despite these challenges, he remained determined to provide for them.

My dad came to America when he was 45 years old. Upon arriving at the JFK Airport in September 1979, he informed his siblings that he considered his offspring his bank account, insinuating that he would work to take care of them. He meant that he would work to educate his children and not worry about maintaining a fat bank account. As an immigrant, he accepted the pains of some low-paying jobs in the chill of New York City to make a living and take care of his kids in Haiti. He did whatever he could to earn income to pay for housing, food, and school for his children and other relatives he left behind in Haiti. He was a brave man and a fighter who always believed in his ability to make things happen.

One of his remarkable accomplishments was obtaining a technical certificate in home maintenance from a technical school in New Jersey at age sixty-five. I am immensely proud that my dad installed new lights for me, renovated one of my bathrooms, laid new floors, and crafted some great cabinets for my garage. He was a consummate professional, always taking pride in his work.

The closing chapter of his life is quite inspiring. He always told his children that education was the only inheritance he would leave for them. Through his lifestyle and resolute mission of promoting education within his family, friends, and home village, he passed on an invaluable legacy to his children. One of the key stories I share in this book serves as a testament to my dad's life. His journey will inspire others to pursue their missions and leave a legacy worth remembering.

The following story occurred when he was in his late seventies, and I consider those events my dad's most important legacy. While he did not leave me and my siblings million-dollar homes on the beach or a private jet, he entrusted us with an asset that will enable us to forge a life capable of making a positive impact on the world and supporting future generations for years to come.

One evening, while in New Jersey, he started feeling sick and went to the emergency room at King County Hospital in Brooklyn, New York. There, the medical team diagnosed him with bradycardia, a condition characterized by a slower-than-usual heart rate. Although the attending cardiologists suggested implanting a pacemaker, he adamantly declined to give consent despite his children's and family's efforts to persuade him. Desperate for more information, I contacted a friend of mine who is a physician. He explained the procedure and provided the pros and cons of having a pacemaker. Convinced of its necessity, I pleaded with my dad to reconsider. However, he confidently dismissed my concerns, asserting that he would seek multiple professional opinions before making a final decision. Despite my efforts, he left the hospital without approving the recommended procedure.

His innate stubbornness and determination to shape his destiny were evident. He never allowed others to influence his decisions. When he took action, it was always because he genuinely wanted to, never succumbing to external pressure.

In 2012, after the pacemaker incident, I had a heart-to-heart conversation with my dad, during which he made a surprising and amusing statement. He mentioned that he didn't want the pacemaker because he believed his health issues stemmed from eating crunchy cornmeal around 10:00 P.M., particularly the crispy bits at the bottom of the pot. He believed eating crunchy cornmeal late at night shouldn't have been the reason to consider getting a pacemaker, as it could affect his ability to interact normally in daily activities. Among those activities, I would include climbing the mountains of his home village of Gros-Saut, Leogane, Haiti.

That event must have sparked a spiritual awakening in my dad. The following year, he made a decision that would mark a significant milestone: returning to Haiti, his homeland, after thirty-four years of living in the U.S. without ever returning. For my dad, Haiti is synonymous with his home village. His dad served as a sheriff there, and he was admired for his leadership and compassionate treatment of others, even while being firm with those who broke the law. This place holds a special significance in my dad's heart—it was like the temple of his soul. He cherished the people who, in turn, admired and respected him. He was captivated by the stories of his family that took place there and the natural beauty of the landscape— the waterfall, the rivers, and the inspiring design of the mountains. He had a special connection with the Catholic chapel, where his dad was the director. Additionally, he loved the local production of fresh, organic produce.

After graduating from elementary school, he was invited to teach at one of the countryside parish schools in his hometown. Regrettably, the advancements in education from his time to the present are minimal; the children lack a suitable building for their classes. The village, under the leadership of Joseph Andre Rosier, a Catholic seminarian at the time and a member of the community, built a school, only for it to be destroyed by the catastrophic 2010 earthquake that devastated Haiti and deeply affected the country. Tragically, state officials show no significant plans for the village's inhabitants—a neglect that extends to much of the country's population. The centralized operations in the capital city have profoundly impacted the countryside's people, who have little to no access to essential services. In honor of my dad's legacy, I have set a personal goal to lead a project to build a school for the village.

Saint Gabriel Catholic Church, a parish in another district of his hometown, oversees the village's elementary school, which is affiliated with the local Catholic church.

Upon returning there after thirty-four years of living in the U.S., he was devastated by the villagers' quality of life. While he could not solve all the village's problems, he established a scholarship program for village children, especially those attending the parish school. Sadly, if parents want to send their kids to secondary school, the equivalent of middle and high school combined in America, they must climb mountains and walk for an hour or more on average.

 He needed to ensure that those with restricted means could go to school. Despite receiving less than $700 in social security benefits and having no real financial assets, he still managed to finance the project. At the age of eighty, my dad was able to help 149 children attend school using his monthly social security benefits, demonstrating that even a modest income couldn't deter him from making a significant impact. He would travel back to Haiti yearly to take care of his project. I remember one day accompanying him as we climbed a mountain named Morne Joseph (Mount Joseph) to visit the parish pastor, who was responsible for the school, to make a payment. While climbing the hill, it was interesting to hear my dad expressing his power, even at eighty years old. As we were climbing the mountain, I was inclined to help him. When I showed him my interest and motivation to give him a hand, he attested that he was still a strong man with no libido problem and no erectile dysfunction. Wow! This was amazing. My eighty-year-old dad was publicizing his strength. As his son, I found it both encouraging and quite amusing to hear him proudly promote the quality of his libido. We arrived at our destination after more than four hours on the road. My dad delivered the payments for the scholarship beneficiaries to the pastor. We couldn't stay long, so we left in less than an hour to take the painful road back home. We departed around 8:00 AM and returned home around 6:00 PM. It is striking how many things are taken for granted by most people in the U.S. I invite you to visit, one day, a place in the world where there is no electricity, no roads for cars, no medical centers, and no easy access to drinking water, among other often overlooked conveniences. Such an experience can be truly enlightening and might change your life forever.

On December 18th, 2022, my dad died at the age of eighty-nine. Now that he is no longer alive, I reflect on his decision to return to his home village right after the doctors suggested implanting a pacemaker in his heart. He must have realized that time was not on his side and that he had to take action to complete his life's mission of advancing the cause of education in his home village. My dad was reputed to be someone who loves education. He has played the role of mentor to many young people who saw him as a role model. Being the son of an ex-sheriff of the village, he was well respected by the residents. He became a benefactor and started the scholarship funding project by recruiting sponsors for the children. His children, siblings, extended relatives, and friends were the team of sponsors he selected to support the children. Sponsoring the children costs a modest yearly donation of $20 per child. Because the school is in the countryside and the parish knows the parents do not have money, they are only required to pay fifty Haitian Gourdes (HTG), less than fifty cents in American currency. However, some parents struggle to afford even this minimal fee or are not motivated to do so. Sometimes, education is not their priority. Nonetheless, I believe the school's schedule and methodology should be adapted to the village's lifestyle, especially considering the economic necessities of agricultural production. Some parents prefer sending their children to work in the gardens instead of sending them to school.

In line with my dad's mission, it was ensured that these children would be afforded the chance to attend school and grasp the essentials of reading, writing, and arithmetic, much like Tyler Perry's Madea would humorously emphasize. In January 2023, the family generously used the remaining funds, collected exclusively from his children for his funeral, to cover seven months of teacher salaries at the school. This assistance enabled the school to maintain its operations, even without payments from parents.

In 2023, the family took full responsibility for the teachers' salaries, which means that my dad was still alive through his mission. His existence remained impactful indeed. Some of my high school classmates collected money during his funeral to support the mission of funding the village's school. By doing that, they attest that they pay tribute to my dad through his mission of supporting education. He will stay alive through his mission. My dad has shown me through his actions that the key to a meaningful life is to embrace a mission and commit to it until it is accomplished. This dedication will be our legacy on earth, which is why the value of our mission can be priceless, as explained in the next section.

Understanding Your Mission's Value

The time you spend finding your mission should be regarded as one of the most critical moments of your life because once you realize you have a mission to fulfill, your life will never be the same. The world faces a multitude of pressing issues, making it impossible to solve them all. The best way to make life meaningful on this planet is to choose one field of intervention or a significant problem and embrace it as your mission. This is the best way to plan your life and live it remarkably. If you want to solve all the issues or problems of this world, you will end up fixing nothing before you transition to the next life.

One life, one mission. You cannot take care of everything. Imagine someone who decides to help every single cause on this planet. Eventually, they will realize that it is impossible to respond to every single depressing ad on TV asking for donations to save a starving child or one species endangered by our irresponsible actions. At some point, the donor will get donor fatigue without being able to measure the impact of their contributions or donations. On the other hand, the donor can concentrate their efforts on one main issue and donate enough to make a significant impact. Even a small donor can make an impact if the focus is solely on one project.

Defining your mission will allow you to live your life with purpose and elevate its significance through your individualized touch. Your mission serves as the very essence of your legacy, planting a lasting impact on the collective memory. Just as Martin Luther King, Franklin D. Roosevelt, and Galileo Galilei are immortalized for their permanent contributions, your accomplished mission symbolizes your everlasting presence.

Your mission is your compass, and your vision relates to the boat's destination.

Live not solely for your job or profession but for your mission. Your work should be a means to support and fulfill that mission, which lies at the essence of your existence. Without this guiding purpose, you risk traveling through life like a lost soul. Your mission constitutes your life's fundamental "why," offering the strength to persevere, especially in challenging times. Friedrich Nietzsche's words resonate with this idea: "He who has a why to live can bear almost any how."[15] A person's mission defines their direction. Please embark on a mission to discover your true purpose on this planet. With your mission as the guiding force, your life will become a rewarding and exciting adventure.

The story of my dad's mission is meaningful in a time when the world needs individuals who can take the lead and contribute to various areas of society, such as healthcare solutions (particularly mental health), economic development, innovation, conflict resolution, job creation, global warming, childcare, mental health, peacebuilding, gun control, education, environmental sustainability, and more.

In this time of spiritual awakening, it is essential to realize that your role is unique. Nobody else can fulfill it or perform it better than you are capable of. Everyone should discern their

---

[15] Frankl, Victor E. Man's Search for Meaning. Beacon Press, 2006, P. 76.

specific role. No one can achieve it as uniquely as you, regardless of intelligence or strength. If you are uncertain about what the universe desires, it is your responsibility to choose your mission.

Today presents the opportunity to discover your true mission and cultivate the determination to achieve it skillfully. The world stands to benefit from your success.

While you may not hear an angelic voice urging you to save your country, recognize that your mission is just as crucial as Joan of Arc's for France's kingdom during the early 1400s. You do not need to save France from English dominance or liberate any other country from colonization, but you can strive to address one of the world's pressing issues currently impacting millions of lives.

You can embark on the journey of enhancing your village's prosperity, elevating the education system, pioneering groundbreaking products to transform our lifestyle or business methods, devising strategies to cultivate youth creativity and commitment to work, constructing support frameworks to assist parents with their duties, or leading initiatives to harmoniously blend artificial intelligence into our daily existence without disrupting our natural progress. The horizon of possibilities is boundless. Sometimes, the inner voice will be like an angel's, begging you to do something about a world-facing problem. If you ever feel that burning desire to intervene and do something, do not resist. The world indeed requires your extraordinary power, the power that you may not be aware of, much like Joan of Arc was not aware of her capacity to bring victory to France and restore the dignity of its kingdom in 1429. You have the mission, but the world is the one that will benefit from its achievement. Do not ever take your mission lightly.

Your mission is as important as winning a world war or solving a pandemic. In fact, you should never doubt the significance of your mission. The world can be described as a system; every part remains as vital as the system itself. Your mission forms a crucial part of that system, and if you neglect your part, the world system will be disrupted.

You are responsible for carrying out your mission with pride and ownership as soon as you have adopted one.

What Is Your Mission?

A clear definition of your mission marks the beginning of a balanced life. Once you define your mission, your life will start making sense. You will feel stronger than ever and equipped to confront life's obstacles. While you will still cherish your bed, you will be thrilled to wake up in the morning and go out to work, not only to better your own life but also to impact other people's lives positively. Your adopted mission with exemplary commitment will bring success, health, happiness, balance, and fulfillment.

By embracing your mission, you tap into your incredible potential. Driven by a commitment to enhancing the well-being of others, your mission reflects your love for life and dedication to making a positive difference in the world.

Be aware that your mission is not your profession. While your profession may be related to or supportive of your mission, they are distinct entities. A profession primarily enables you to earn a livelihood, whereas your mission involves addressing issues more significant than your personal or familial concerns. Your mission should never be centered around personal problems but should extend to improving the world. The scope of a personal mission goes beyond the individual ego. It is a statement about your life's worth to the world, humanity, or the universe. For example, having a house on the beach is not a mission. Conversely, raising awareness about ocean pollution can be your personal mission.

Your personal mission extends beyond your individual welfare. It encompasses a commitment to improving the world. It specifies how you intend to address the challenges facing communities, cities, states, countries, villages, continents, races, humanity, or even the universe.

A true mission is never solely about personal gain. If it becomes so, it ceases to be a mission and instead becomes a desire or goal to improve your life. Sadhguru, the renowned Indian guru, has clarified the distinction between desire and vision. In one of the YouTube videos he is featured in, he teaches that a desire pertains to personal aspirations, while a vision is focused on realizing societal impact. I embrace Sadhguru's distinction, even though he uses the term 'vision,' because, in this book, 'vision' represents a tangible aspiration for a mission. Your mission transcends your individual existence; it is a commitment to something greater than yourself. This is why having a mission is crucial. It enables you to optimize your potential by working not only for personal gain but also for the betterment of the world. Your mission embodies a testament to your love for life and your dedication to improving the lives of others.

Your mission is an amplification of yourself, surpassing your individual identity. Just as a scientist instantly connects 'alternating current' with Nikola Tesla for his remarkable contributions or 'direct current' with Thomas Edison, your mission embodies your life's essence.

It reflects the core of who you are and serves as the true definition of your identity. It defines your uniqueness.

Your Uniqueness Makes You Special

Think of your mission as the building block that defines your specialty and makes you unique. Your mission tells the world who you are and why you are alive. Life can seem senseless without that mission—like an airplane flying without a destination.

You have a special gift that makes you unique. If you have siblings, you'll notice that each one has a set of talents that make them different from the rest. Uniqueness starts in our DNA composition. When siblings are born, they inherit only 50% of their parents' DNA, making each one distinct. We are different from one another right from birth, with different qualities, strengths, and weaknesses. Even identical twins will differ due to environmental and circumstantial factors, resulting in unique contributions to the world.

Take pleasure in showcasing the marvels of your uniqueness and specialty to the world.

Mission vs. Profession

You should establish the difference between your profession and your mission. Your job or profession may serve as a means of fulfilling your mission. However, your job is not necessarily your mission. You can have a dozen jobs in your lifetime but only one true mission. There is a clear distinction between the two. Your mission is a primary goal set for your life, and you have the sacred obligation to determine what that mission is. Searching for your mission is akin to searching for your true self. That quest allows you to rediscover yourself. When you clearly understand your mission, you are on your way to making a unique contribution to humanity's welfare. Without that mission, you may take any job or embark on any project without knowing your destination; you will embrace every endeavor without a clear purpose for your life's journey. Your job or profession helps strengthen your mission's foundation. Your mission defines you, while your job reflects your current situation. Your mission is permanent, whereas your job is temporary. By having a clear path for your life's journey, guided by your well-understood mission, your direction is set regarding what you value in life and how you can make your existence worthwhile. Your mission serves as a guiding light for your actions, endeavors, and projects. You have a legacy to build, which will be valuable only if a well-defined mission guides you.

Your work is a means of survival. Your profession or trade helps you secure a job or provide a service to meet your immediate needs. The primary function of your profession or job is to help you survive as an individual. Your job addresses short-term needs, while your mission aims to solve long-term issues. I consider your mission as spiritual and your job as material. Your mission is idealistic, while your job is realistic. You ensure that you secure a job that can at least cover all your bills and provide a little extra for rainy days. Your mission, on the other hand, does not solely consider the reality you are currently living in as the main criterion for selection. If you delve into your inner universe, you may discover a mission that transcends your current capacity. The story of Joan of Arc elegantly illustrates the potential of a mission that surpasses the imagination of the individual tasked with carrying it out. That is what you are meant to achieve. Your life's central goal has little to do with your current state. Your DNA may hold the essence of your mission, while your job is influenced by the environment in which you live. Your mission nurtures your love for humanity, while your job primarily caters to your ego, the little me. You may see little value in working hard until you integrate a mission into your daily activities. Taking your mission seriously will help you reach peak performance in your job or profession. When you identify your true mission, you will not only add meaning to your life but also embark on a journey of personal growth and self-discovery.

Your mission will help you add a sense to your life and bring meaning to your existence. You will become balanced when you harmonize your job and life's true purpose. Therefore, your profession or your work should be linked to your mission. If your job is part of your overall mission, you will display satisfaction, positively affecting your balance and happiness. I understand you cannot neglect the urgent need to pay your bills and bring food to the table, but you must envision your long-term goals. If you ever have a job you do not like, you should have your mission in sight until you find the one that allows you to accomplish it. You should be incredibly careful when choosing a job that does not coordinate with your mission. The average time you spend in a job is eight hours a day. You should add an average of two hours of preparation to the calculation for those not working from home. If you spend eight hours a day plus two hours of preparation for five days doing something that brings no personal satisfaction, it is almost certain that you will experience an imbalance in your life. People are often running after well-paid jobs. Don't get me wrong, I personally want a highly lucrative job or enterprise. This is a wonderful goal, and there is nothing wrong with the desire to find a job with satisfactory compensation. However, working for a meaningful mission can be more beneficial overall. Look for well-paid jobs that allow you to stay healthy and take care of your mission. Many professionals struggle with their overall health, especially their mental health, because they have been chasing money and neglecting their meaningful mission for too long.

Even though there may be other causes of a mid-life crisis, don't be surprised if this personal life issue is closely related to a mismatch between what we do for a living and what our real mission should be. If your job aligns with your mission, you rarely feel bored or tired because your commitment will give you strength and perseverance. Mid-life crises sometimes occur because a person's job does not allow them to fulfill their mission or because they don't feel they are contributing to something valuable according to their perceptions.

Imagine a world where everyone assumes full responsibility for pursuing and fulfilling their life's mission, enhancing the collective experience for everyone. If everyone believes that they have a specific role to exercise, this world will be a million times better than what we have now, and it is almost impossible to imagine all the things that humanity would have accomplished with this type of behavior. When a person's mission is taken seriously, numerous opportunities and possibilities arise to benefit from. The story of Joan of Arc can be inspiring even though some people attribute her accomplishments to some supernatural capacity. I use her story as an example because it encourages you to listen to that inner voice, urging you to recognize and pursue your mission, and assuring you that you can achieve it.

How to Find Your Mission?

Searching for your mission is comparable to searching for your soul. Your body is a temporary and fragile entity. The physical portion of yourself and its materialistic realizations are for a brief period. As you know, life is simply short. Only your mission, once materialized, can make you last more than a lifetime. Your mission is the eternal light of your life. Your mission is what makes your life permanent. How to search for your mission is a tricky question. I do not think anyone has the magic bullet for you to determine what your mission is. However, we can set some general guidelines on how to find your life's mission.

The first step in determining your life's mission is to cultivate self-awareness. Stay in touch with your inner voice, know your strengths and weaknesses, connect with your roots by understanding your family background and values, and recognize how you respond to different circumstances in your environment.

In some instances, your inner voice will dictate your mission. You will naturally feel motivated toward certain events or projects, developing a special interest in a particular activity or issue. I vividly remember a moment during a church service when I suddenly felt a calling to become a priest. While priesthood in a specific religion may not be my path now, I am confident that my mission lies in using my inspiration to motivate people to take action and improve their lives. Since then, I have been speaking publicly, finding fulfillment in motivating others. I discovered my mission at age eleven and have lived accordingly ever since.

My journey began when I talked to a group at a meeting for young people in the Catholic Church's 'Holy Family' group. My composure and proficiency amazed me while explaining a biblical passage to my peers. At fourteen, I spoke in front of a large crowd in a neighborhood of Port-au-Prince, attempting to convert people to Christianity. Although my views on religion have evolved, these experiences shaped my mission of speaking to improve lives. However, not everyone finds their mission as easily. Meditation, prayer, and affirmations can be helpful, but not everyone follows that path. Therefore, I've included two exercises at the end of this chapter to aid in determining the mission you wish to pursue. Ultimately, I am convinced that it is your responsibility to decide your life's path, whether or not you believe in a supernatural entity.

Meditation, affirmations, and prayers allow you to connect with your inner voice, which can put you in the right direction when trying to find your mission. I want to draw the differences between meditation, prayer, and affirmation. In meditation, the subject listens to Universal Intelligence in inner peace. On the other hand, in a prayer, the subject speaks to God or Universal Intelligence. When I evoke the term meditation, I mean transcendental meditation. On the Cleveland Clinic's website, it is defined as a meditation technique where you mentally repeat a word or phrase until you reach a state of inner peace.[16] I have been exposed to this technique since I was in high school.

---

[16] Cleveland Clinic. "Transcendental Meditation." Cleveland Clinic, Accessed March 18, 2024.
https://my.clevelandclinic.org/health/treatments/22292-transcendental-meditation.

You do not need to be a believer to meditate because the goal is to get to a point where you have no thoughts or words. The difference between prayers and affirmations is that in prayers, the subject addresses their request to an entity they believe in, while in affirmations, the subject speaks their wants or desires to the universe, imprinting the desired state in the subconscious mind. Affirmations are positive statements that are meant to be repeated multiple times, just like a mantra. A mantra is a word or phrase repeated over and over to cultivate focus and a sense of direction in someone's life. For example, if you want peace in your life, you can repeat the word peace for a certain period to build a peaceful life for yourself. While a mantra is mostly a single word and an affirmation is a statement, both serve a similar purpose. They aim to guide the subconscious mind towards the desired outcomes in one's life. Mantras and affirmations help clarify and reinforce what the individual wishes to manifest or achieve. I do not want this book to direct you to a specific religion in any way. I am convinced that everyone can find their life's true mission regardless of religion or spiritual position, including those who say they do not believe. Unbelievably, everyone should have a mission to fulfill on this planet. The brain is so powerful that we should make our lives count for some extraordinary things. Committing ourselves to a specific mission allows the world to take full advantage of the gift we represent. We should respect each other's positions, beliefs, and choices. We can work together for a better world without regard to race, gender, color, beliefs, customs, and personal preferences. If everyone is committed to a personal mission to improve the quality of life, the world will flourish.

Another way to determine your mission is to list all the gifts in your life. What's your vocation? Ask yourself: What am I gifted for? As students excel in math, literature, art, or sports, understanding your strengths can help uncover your life's purpose. However, it's important to note that while selecting a profession may align with your gifts, it may not necessarily encompass your mission, as I mentioned earlier.

The third method involves inventorying the world's various challenges and identifying which ones resonate with your values and personal motivation. Some individuals naturally gravitate towards specific areas of life such as healthcare, education, childcare, or family life.

Regardless of your personal mission, its value lies in its potential to foster positive change in the world. However, commitment is essential for your mission to hold significance. Your mission may even become more important than your personal life. Numerous world leaders, including Nelson Mandela, Indira Gandhi, Martin Luther King Jr., Abraham Lincoln, and countless others, have exemplified the transformative power of a personal mission.

Ikigai: The Japanese concept for life's mission

Every year, November 11th is significant in my life as it marks my dad's birthday. In 2023, this day became even more emotional as it marked his first birthday since his passing in December 2022. The occasion compelled me to reflect on my life's mission and my dad's profound role in my achievements. This introspection made me reconnect with past mentors from Edmonds Community College in Lynnwood, Washington, where I earned an associate degree and multiple diplomas in 1995.

Among these mentors was Marion Weldon, a remarkable woman and my former instructor in human resource management and other business management classes. Mrs. Weldon, now a certified career-life transformational consultant, played a crucial role in coaching me throughout the book-writing process. A Google search reunited us, and after several exchanges, I invited Mrs. Marion to write the foreword for this book. as she was the person who first introduced me to the concept of a personal mission through a video program featuring Jack Canfield titled "Self-Esteem and Peak Performance." Jack Canfield, a renowned speaker and author in personal development, inspired me to focus on the importance of defining one's personal mission. I am thrilled to acknowledge and honor Marion's contribution to my career, especially in completing my first published book.

In December 2023, Mrs. Weldon shared a link introducing me to the concept of Ikigai. After I read the content on Ikigai, I concluded that it was necessary to include the concept of Ikigai in my book on *success with meaning*. Ikigai comprises two Japanese words: "iki" (life) and "gai" (value). It is regarded as one's reason for being. French speakers like me would say: raison d'être (the reason why someone or something exists). Seeking to provide clarity to my Facebook platform, I consulted my Japanese friend Takeo Uchiyama, a former student advisor for Japanese students at Edmonds Community College, to define Ikigai. According to Mr. Takeo Uchiyama, Ikigai is "to feel fulfilling one's mission in life." This definition resonated with his Japanese friends, although his eighty-eight-year-old mother-in-law pointed out that *Ikigai* can evolve over the years, embodying what motivates you to wake up every morning and engage in work and responsibilities.

My initial encounter with Takeo at Edmonds Community College in 1994 left a lasting impression when he commended me for my smile, recognizing it as an expression of personal evolution. It became clear that he saw in me a realization of Ikigai – the sense of fulfilling one's life mission, radiating energy, balance, and happiness to the world. Helping others discover their missions can contribute to addressing mental health issues worldwide. When you identify and act on your true mission, you will embark on a transformative journey, displaying positive energy and freedom from anxiety. It is worth noting that Okinawa, Japan, stands as the origin of Ikigai and is recognized as a blue zone city. Blue zones[17] are regions where a notable proportion of individuals live beyond one hundred years.

---

[17] Forbes Health. "Blue Zones in the US: What Are They and Why Are They Important?" Forbes, March 6, 2024.
https://www.forbes.com/health/nutrition/blue-zones-in-the-us/#:~:text=Simply%20put%2C%20blue%20zones%20are,term%20blue%20zones%20in%202004.

In effect, having a sense of purpose remains one of the characteristics often observed in blue zones. I believe that discovering your Ikigai can contribute to an extended and healthy life, coupled with a profound sense of accomplishment.

The Ikigai philosophy revolves around four core elements: Mission, Passion, Vocation, and Profession[18]. Coincidentally, the MVP-PA success model, which stands for Mission, Vision, Passion, Plan, and Action, shares many similarities with Ikigai, leading me to think of it as "Ikigai plus." This alignment is entirely coincidental, as I never encountered the concept of Ikigai before Mrs. Marion shared the link with me. According to the Ikigai philosophy, finding your Ikigai involves establishing a balanced connection with your mission (what the world needs), passion (what you love to do), vocation (what you are good at), and profession (what you are paid for). The MVP-PA success model considers mission and passion as two crucial elements of *success with meaning*, eventually leading you to a balanced life. Additionally, the exercises at the end of this chapter suggest that you consider your gifted skills (vocation) when defining your mission. You will have a balanced life if you integrate your mission, vocation, and passion into your profession or everyday life. Inspired by the Ikigai philosophy, we can define a fantastic job or enterprise as an opportunity you are passionate about, allowing you to leverage your gifts or vocation, practice your profession, and fulfill your mission. Upon completing this book, I hope you discover your *Ikigai*, aligning with your

---

[18] Héctor García and Francesc Miralles, Ikigai: The Japanese Secret to a Long and Happy Life (New York: Penguin Books, 2016), p. 12

mission and paving the way for a balanced life. The MVP-PA success model will be valuable for constructing a successful and fulfilling life.

The next section will provide more details on Viktor Frankl's concept of logotherapy. Although I previously discussed Frankl in the chapter on personal responsibility, I did not delve into logotherapy. Now, I will explore its connection to the teachings of the ikigai philosophy and the MVP-PA success model.

Ikigai and Logotherapy

If you take classes on Ikigai, especially in Western environments, they tend to have a chapter on logotherapy by Victor Frankl. The reason is that logotherapy deals directly with meaning, which has a direct connection with life's mission. I personally define mission as the ultimate meaning of someone's life. People will find their life's purpose or mission when looking for meaning. Victor Frankl was a holocaust survivor who invented a new concept of psychotherapy called logotherapy. Logotherapy comes from two words: "logos," a Greek word for meaning, and "therapy," which means healing. Basically, logotherapy means therapy through meaning. In logotherapy[19], the therapist tries to heal the neurotic patient in attempting to help them find meaning in their lives. Viktor Frankl, in his innovative approach to psychotherapy, suggests that finding meaning in life is an effective solution to mental health issues[20].

Victor Frankl employs existential analysis as a therapeutic tool, underscoring the notion that an existential vacuum may precipitate depression, aggression, or addiction. "Such widespread phenomena as depression, aggression, and addiction are not understandable unless we recognize the existential underlying them."[21] - Victor Frankl.

---

[19] WebMD, accessed January 31, 2024, "What Is Logotherapy?" https://www.webmd.com/mental-health/what-is-logotherapy.

[20] Frankl, Viktor E. *Man's Search for Meaning*. Boston: Beacon Press, 2006.

[21] Viktor E. Frankl, "Man's Search for Meaning." Beacon Press, 2006, p. 107.

To remedy these potential deficiencies, individuals can proactively seek meaning in their lives, diminishing the impact of the existential void, and mitigating the risk of severe emotional challenges. Frankl introduces the concept of transcendence—a profound motivation for individuals to dedicate themselves to a cause or the well-being of others.

It is noteworthy that when Dr. Frankl delves into the theme of meaning, the pursuit thereof becomes an ongoing exercise. Humans engage in a perpetual quest for significance in every impactful life event, fostering a more positive outlook over time. In this context, we can regard our mission as a long-term constituent of our lives, while meaning can be dissected through short-term analyses. Within Frankl's logotherapy, meaning and purpose emerge as pivotal concepts, shaping the framework for a fulfilled existence. In his book "The Pursuit of Meaning," Joseph Fabry sums up Victor Frankl's central philosophy on meaning: "To Frankl, our basic motivation for living is not to find pleasure, power or material riches but to find meaning."[22]

Victor Frankl adheres to existentialism, a philosophy asserting that existence precedes essence. This perspective emphasizes individuals' fundamental free will and capacity to shape their destinies. Frankl reinforces that we must actively identify our life's purpose and explore its meaning rather than passively allowing genetic factors, environmental influences, or external circumstances to dictate our path. He urges us to take charge of defining our personal mission and underscores that the

---

[22] Joseph B. Fabry, "The Pursuit of Meaning." Purpose Research (2013): p. 14.

responsibility for discovering it lies solely within ourselves. According to The Ethics Center, existentialism is the philosophical belief that "we are each responsible for creating purpose or meaning in our own lives."23

It is important to note that existentialists can be both believers and non-believers. They agree on the fact that human beings should take control of their destinies by taking responsibility and action for what they want to achieve.

The term self-made properly matches the philosophy of existentialism because it refers to people who have earned their success through hard work and self-determination. Their success is not dictated by their essence but rather by their ability to act on their existence. I urge you to be a self-made individual. Act daily to defy the odds and achieve success by discovering your mission and working towards its realization.

In his presentations, including his book titled *Man's Search for Meaning*, Viktor Frankl extensively explores the concept of the existential vacuum, describing it as a state of inner emptiness and meaninglessness. He has mentioned that this existential vacuum often occurs during significant life transitions or when individuals confront existential questions about the meaning of life.

---

[23] The Ethics Centre. "Existentialism Explainer." Accessed January 31, 2024. https://ethics.org.au/ethics-explainer-existentialism/#:~:text=Existentialism%20is%20the%20philosophical%20belief,governments%2C%20teachers%20or%20other%20authorities.

Embarking on a search for meaning, an excellent starting point in finding one's lifelong mission, remedies this existential void.

As the founder of the third Viennese school of psychotherapy, Frankl underscores the individual's motivation to attain a certain level of transcendence—a dedication to a specific cause or the well-being of a particular person. Happiness is consequently regarded as a by-product of transcendence. Logotherapy is the third Viennese school of psychotherapy due to Vienna, Austria, being the birthplace of two earlier psychotherapeutic theories. According to Victor Frankl, Sigmund Freud's initial theory concluded that human motivation primarily stems from the will to pleasure. In contrast, Alfred Adler's theory, also originating from Vienna, revolves around the will to power arising from the cultivation of an inferiority complex at an early age, compelling individuals to seek power as compensation for perceived inferiority.

Victor Emil Frankl, the author of the book titled "Man's Search for Meaning," revolutionized the field of psychotherapy by emphasizing the search for meaning as the individual's primary motivation. Constantly seeking ways to address daily challenges, humanity finds its most effective approach through a continuous quest for answers. The evolution of psychotherapy across these three Viennese schools of thought has empowered humanity to discover viable solutions to life challenges and mental health issues. Logotherapy continues to help individuals uncover meaning in their lives through dynamic dialogues.

Even though the primary goal of my writing is to focus on success, I am excited to connect the notions of mission and health by delving into the concept of meaning articulated by Victor Frankl. My satisfaction deepens further upon considering the statement made by Joseph B. Fabry regarding the pursuit of meaning and peak experiences: "If we devote ourselves to the pursuit of meaning, our lives are full of meaning and the by-products of a meaningful existence: happiness, security, peace of mind, mental stability, and such currently fashionable life goals as self-actualization and peak experiences."[24]

---

[24] Joseph B. Fabry, *The Pursuit of Meaning* (Purpose Research, 2013), p. 71.

Examples of Mission Statements

These mission statements represent a wide array of personal missions, all dedicated to addressing various societal, environmental, and humanitarian challenges. Each statement embodies an individual's commitment to driving positive change within their specific sphere of influence.

- Minimizing the effects of global warming through enhanced education and information dissemination.
- Protecting wildlife.
- Promoting a balanced family life.
- Improving educational systems, both in the US and worldwide.
- Enhancing the quality of construction in impoverished nations.
- Ensuring equitable access to quality healthcare for all Americans.
- Safeguarding children worldwide through improved health, education, and family support.
- Addressing the needs of adoption processes.
- Protecting the lives and well-being of young people globally.
- Promoting higher education opportunities within marginalized communities.
- Inspiring a love for learning, particularly in mathematics and other subjects, among young children.
- Reforming immigration systems to ensure fairness and efficiency.

- Innovating solutions to global peace challenges through product development.
- Seeking viable solutions to public health issues.
- Enhancing healthcare quality, whether in America or elsewhere.
- Improving the lives of children under foster care.
- Enhancing the quality of care provided to seniors in nursing homes.
- Supporting disabled individuals in achieving balanced and fulfilling lives.
- Establishing support networks for those affected by mental health issues.
- Pursuing breakthroughs in treating diseases such as Alzheimer's and cancer.
- Promoting public awareness and education on 21st-century healthcare practices.
- Balancing technology usage with family life for healthier lifestyles.
- Supporting underserved children in communities worldwide.
- Providing access to advanced technologies for children in African American communities.
- Empowering children with decision-making skills for positive interactions.
- Encouraging high school graduation rates among all students.
- Assisting individuals in discovering their life's true purpose.
- Working towards reducing crime rates, both domestically and globally.

- Developing innovative products to enhance quality of life.
- Enhancing customer service standards in various sectors.
- Implementing systemic improvements in customer service on a global scale.
- Strengthening international organizations for greater efficacy.
- Promoting positive parenting practices in America.
- Fostering improved communication within local communities.
- Promoting inclusivity and integration within church communities.
- These mission statements aptly illustrate individuals' purposes based on their diverse passions and commitments, aiming to drive positive change and improve the world.

Do not feel guilty for not embracing every issue on earth. Concentrate on one mission. The key to leaving a legacy for humanity or the universe is to adopt a particular issue and make it your mission. You can never fix all the problems of this world, but you can choose an issue and work to fix it at least partially. Your solutions may not be complete, but the planet will commemorate your accomplishments and preserve your legacy.

Below are the step 1 exercises designed to help you find your mission. The next chapter will explain the concept of vision in detail, allowing you to write a vision statement for your mission.

Step 1 Exercises

Exercise # 1: Craft Your Mission

1. ***List Your Skills***

   List the skills that you consider yourself gifted at.

2. ***Identify Your Strengths***

   List your strengths as a student or a professional.

3. ***Identify Issues***

   Write about an issue in your environment or the world dear to your heart.

4. ***Review Personal Stories***

   Review your personal life stories. Has any story caught your attention? Could one of them help you define your mission? What life story has significantly affected your life?

5. ***Identify Potential Areas***

   Pick two or three areas that could become your mission.

6. ***Assess Passion***

   Review your passion for the selected areas.

7. ***Select Primary Motivation***

   Pick the one that motivates you the most.

Today, you cannot only think about your little world. Humanity has too many people suffering from starvation, injustice, discrimination, health issues, lack of education, lack of access to drinking water, animal deprivation, environmental issues, global warming, war, gun violence, etc. You will achieve more if you think of the world as a bigger you. Start thinking of yourself as part of a system. When one part does not work in a system, the complete system shuts down until that defective part is repaired or replaced. The COVID-19 crisis is considered an opportunity for spiritual awakening because this generation can finally understand, at least for those who can comprehend the scope of the issue, that we are no longer separated and disconnected. We are part of one big world, and nobody can undo what has already been completed. If someone does not want all countries to work together for a better world, they will destroy the world, including their country. We are part of one big family, and you must play your part. We have an extensive list of problems to solve. You must pick yours and play your role with grace and a keen sense of responsibility to make things better for all of us. I urge you to make the world a better place simply by discovering your life's mission and dedicating yourself to it. You can achieve this through education, disseminating information, fostering economic development, creating jobs, providing motivation, and more. Embrace your mission with enthusiasm. If everyone plays their part, the world will undoubtedly become a better place.

Exercise #2

1. ***Listen to Your Inner Voice***
   Take an hour to listen to your inner voice through meditation or silence of your intellect. Be receptive.

2. ***Identify Your "Whys"***
   List five reasons that justify your motivation in life.
   - What drives your quest for phenomenal success?
   - What motivates you to wake up to work or start your business activities daily?
   - Is a specific reason, besides paying the bills, inspiring you to work harder than your peers?
   - Are there organizations that ignite your life's passion?
   - Are there individuals or groups motivating you to grow and help them?

   Please note that your 'whys' are your life motivators. They are meant to justify your passion and drive.

Context Example

A worker in a respirator manufacturing plant serves as a compelling example. This individual contributes to their family's well-being and saves lives by producing respirators for COVID-19 cases and other respiratory diseases. Similarly, consider a life insurance agent who earns commissions by bringing new customers to insurance companies. Aiding families during sickness or death is a significant motivation for such professionals. Workers who understand the true purpose behind their roles tend to excel in the marketplace.

3. *Identify Important Issues*

Name three national or international issues that are important to you.

4. *Identify Your Core Values*

What do you value the most besides your personal life and family?

(Justice, education, world peace, integrity, moral values, love, charity, personal responsibility, wildlife, communication, conflict resolution, mental health, spirituality, patriotism, etc.)

5. *Craft Your Mission Statement*

Try to write your mission statement based on your answers to questions 1 to 4. Keep it simple

Chapter 5
Step 2: Develop a Personal Vision Statement

"In order to carry a positive action, we must develop here a positive vision."[25]

– Dalai Lama

In the vision stage, as the architect of your personal achievement, you are transforming your dream related to your mission into a tangible aspiration. This is not a small goal but a proposition representing the ideal realization of your mission—an aspiration worth striving for, one that may extend beyond a single lifetime. Achieving your vision requires significant investments of time, resources, intellect, and energy.

Your vision is an ideal yet concrete expression of your mission, providing a clear framework for building a plan of

---

[25] Dalai Lama. " In order to carry a positive action, we must develop here a positive vision." BrainyQuote. Accessed October 29, 2023. https://www.brainyquote.com/quotes/dalai_lama_446740.

action. This vision stems from a big dream. To illustrate the power of such dreams, I have chosen to open this chapter with a poem I wrote over 20 years ago. Big dreams fuel big projects, significant successes, and extraordinary achievements.

This chapter aims to help you grasp the function of vision in the achievement process and equip you with the necessary elements to craft a vision statement for your life's mission that calls for a definitive action plan.

Dreams: A Poetic Introduction

Dreams

They have no colors

They are raceless

Everyone can dream

Leaving aside origin and position

Reality comes from dreams

We are all part of a dream

As we all come from a dream.

And we are as big as the dreams of our lives

Should you stop dreaming

You will cease living

Keep dreaming

Til the dream of your life has ceased.

You are as beautiful as the dream of your life

As wonderful as the dream you are

As strong as your present dream

As happy as the dreams you nurture

Keep dreaming

You'll be surprised to see the power of dreams.

You are nothing but dreams

Your dreams mirror the landscape of your life.

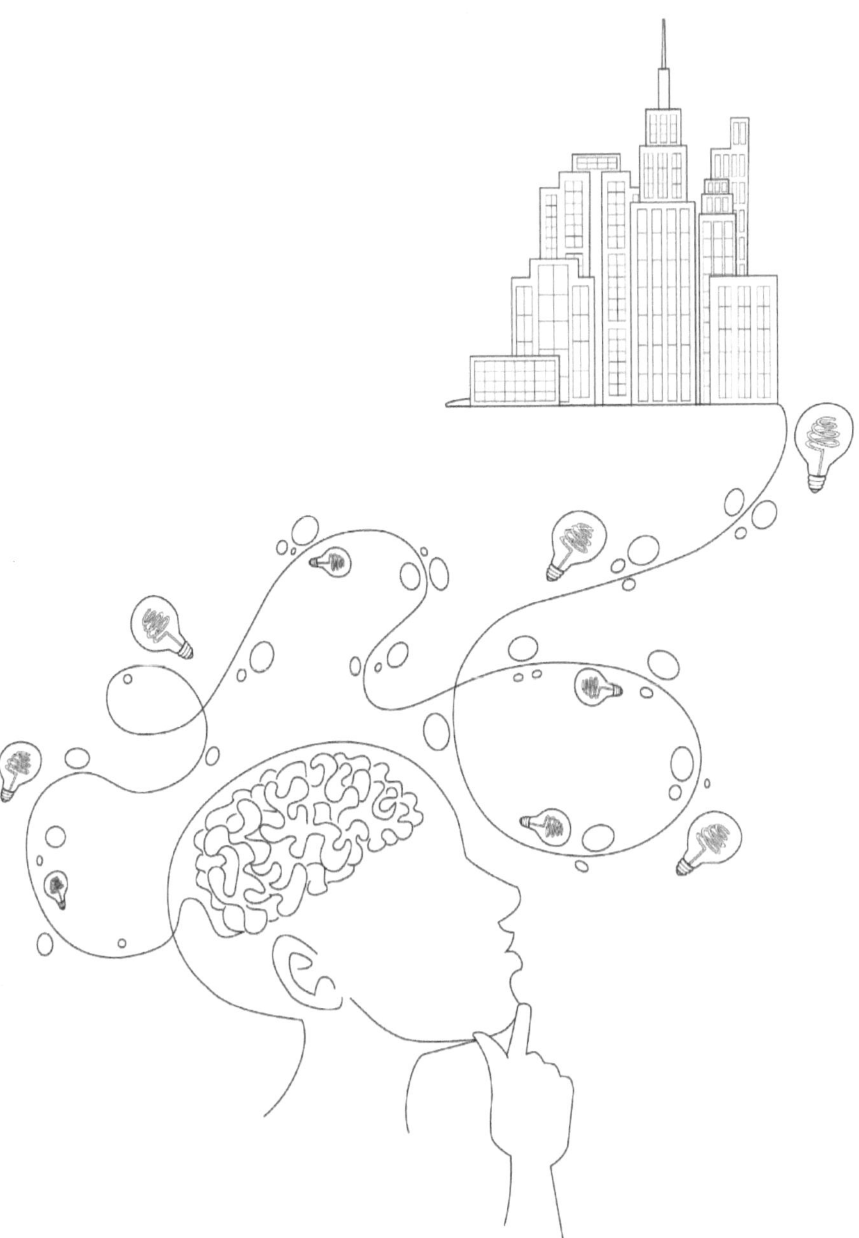

5 *Vision: Aspirations and Transformations that Matter.*

Envisioning Success: Defining the Role of Vision in Realizing Your Mission

Your mission is the lifelong path you choose to follow. Together with your vision, it forms the core of your primary aspirations. The key distinction between a dream and a vision lies in their clarity and concreteness. While a dream often appears indistinct and vague, a vision offers a clearer, more tangible form of this dream. It serves as the initial step towards dedication, establishing a concrete goal that initiates the process of turning your dream into an achievable reality.

It is important to note that our approach to personal vision slightly deviates from the commonly accepted definition. Consider this definition by Giulia Bastoni: "A personal vision statement describes your personal values, strengths, and goals. It can focus on life or professional goals and is intended to orient you toward your long-term dreams."[26] While this perspective presents the personal vision statement as a broad concept that encompasses your personal life, our approach adopts a more business-oriented perspective. In this book, you will develop a vision statement intricately linked to a personal mission statement you crafted as the principal dream of your life. The objective is for you to laser-focus on a primary field, serving as a guiding compass. This approach of personal vision statement is directly connected to the mission statement, focusing on what is most crucial.

---

[26] Imbastoni, Giulia. "What Is a Personal Vision Statement?" BetterUp. Accessed April 21, 2024. https://www.betterup.com/blog/create-a-personal-vision-statement#what-is-a-personal-vision-statement.

In 2002, after obtaining a Microsoft certification, I penned the poem "Dreams." Reflecting on countless opportunities before me, I realized the profound value of dreams in shaping our lives. Dreams expand our horizons, allowing us to transcend our limitations and envision a reality greater than our current circumstances. Like all my previous achievements, my success in the certification exam is closely tied to my aspirations of achieving my dreams and ultimately reaching my success goals. Dreams, though abstract, lay the groundwork for our personal vision statements—a more concrete and direct product of our dreams. For this book, whenever we use the term "vision," we are referring to a statement connected to a life's mission.

Life often starts with a vague idea, which evolves into a dream and eventually becomes a project. Each project develops its own mission, guiding its evolution. Our life's mission sets the course of our existence, outlining the fields or areas where we will make a personal impact. In contrast, the vision delineates the scope of your work or intervention within that field, capturing the essence of your aspirations related to your personal mission. Whether you aim to enhance the quality of your field of intervention or expand access to more people, your vision ultimately determines the magnitude and nature of your impact.

The vision precisely quantifies and expands on the mission, enabling you to measure its value in both qualitative and quantitative terms. It then defines the scope of your mission-focused interventions. Guided by your mission, this vision articulates your aspirations regarding the mission's fulfillment.

Once a personal mission is articulated, defining its breadth and depth is crucial. The vision communicates to both you and the world the extent of your commitment to achieving your mission. It reflects both the effort you are willing to invest and the measurable impact you aim to achieve. For example, a college student might decide that their mission is to contribute to people's well-being in the medical field. The medical field embodies the essence of their mission, outlining the specific area where they aim to make an impact. The vision will then delineate the "how," "how much," and "how far." Suppose the mission specifies becoming a physician to deliver care directly. In that case, the vision might detail the number of people or regions the student aims to positively impact through their medical interventions. Similarly, if the visionary individual opts to be a facilitator rather than a direct healthcare provider, that role also falls under their vision's directive.

In a vision statement, you define the scope of your intervention—whether it's impacting your family, village, city, country, race, continent, or even the world. You are the architect of your destiny, tasked with deciding how far you want to go in executing your mission.

Just as a country's greatness mirrors its leaders' vision, an individual's success is shaped by the breadth of their vision. Significant achievements stem from bold visions. At this stage, limitations should be cast aside. Do not let limiting beliefs, such as the idea that current financial constraints prevent you from aiming to help a million people, restrict your vision for your life and your contribution to humanity's future. Your present circumstances should not confine your aspirations; only your mind can create real barriers.

Remember, you are not alone in executing your life's mission. While some may advise you to be realistic, consider that Americans might never have reached the moon if President Kennedy had limited his vision for America's space exploration. This principle of transcending immediate realities is not confined to modern leaders or Western contexts. Turning our gaze to a different era and region, whenever I talk about vision, Haiti's only king, Henry I, comes to mind. His extraordinary vision from the early 1800s continues to benefit Haiti through the Citadelle Laferrière. This mountaintop fortress[27], built in 1813 under the king's leadership near the city of Cap-Haitian, could host up to 5,000 soldiers. King Henry I, who occupied the Northern part of Haiti after 1806, built the "Citadel" to protect his kingdom against potential attacks by foreign forces, especially the French army. As a newly independent nation that gained its independence through a triumphant battle of slaves against Napoleon's French army in 1803, Haiti had to build military infrastructures to protect its territory. The king demonstrated his visionary capacity through this magnificent construction, which is considered a World Heritage Site by UNESCO today. Being pragmatic is valuable, but when your vision is tied too closely to reality, it can impose unnecessary constraints on achieving your mission. You are encouraged to envision a future that extends far beyond your current status or situation. Do not plan based solely on the resources immediately at hand. Many opportunities can be unlocked with a proposal, a letter, a conversation, or a networking event. Embrace

---

[27] UNESCO World Heritage Centre. "National History Park – Citadel, Sans Souci, Ramiers." Accessed June 15, 2024. https://whc.unesco.org/en/list/180/.

audacity and aspire to achievements that go beyond your everyday reality.

Although I was raised in a poor neighborhood of Port-au-Prince, Haiti's capital city, I never allowed myself to dream small. In school, I consistently aimed high, which propelled me to work harder and study more diligently than most students. Early on, I dreamed of impacting the world through aspirational positions in international organizations. Over time, these aspirations broadened, evolving into a vision to influence every city, country, and continent through my lectures, writings, and artworks, aiming to inspire people worldwide toward personal growth.

Although my dad never officially articulated a vision statement for his commitment to advancing education, he fostered a distinct and resolute vision: to guarantee that every child in his village could access educational opportunities. Consequently, he limited the scope of his vision to the village, setting a focused and achievable goal. Inspired by my dad's dedication, others might extend this vision to encompass every child in their city or county. Personal vision statements like these define individuals and shape the extent of their commitment and the energy they intend to dedicate toward achieving their goals.

Your vision delineates the scope of your mission, enabling you to realize your goals and aspirations across varying scales— from your village to the entire world or tailored to specific groups such as your country or ethnicity. It encompasses the extent of your mission's impact, including the number of individuals you aim to influence. For instance, someone might envision making education more affordable across America while preserving the quality of education for future generations. This vision frames the long-term goal and shapes the strategies for achieving substantial and meaningful progress, as explored in the following examples.

Examples of Vision Statements Related to Missions Focusing on Healthcare

- **Healthcare Education:** Bring access to healthcare education to underprivileged communities.
- **Enhance Healthcare Accessibility:** Build state-of-the-art healthcare facilities in various cities nationally and globally.
- **Bring Healthcare to Other Parts of the World:** Extend affordable healthcare services to underserved regions in other continents.
- **Find a Cure for Major Diseases:** Aim to discover affordable cures for major diseases such as Alzheimer's, cancer, and diabetes to reduce the number of affected patients in the targeted areas.
- **Create Vaccines for Pandemic-Level Diseases:** Develop vaccines to combat and prevent spreading pandemic-level diseases.
- **Help Millions Have Access to Quality Healthcare:** Provide one billion people with access to quality healthcare services based on pre-established healthcare service quality metrics.
- **Improve Healthcare Delivery:** Enhance the efficiency and effectiveness of healthcare delivery systems in your country.
- **Reduce Healthcare Costs:** Work towards significantly lowering healthcare expenses nationally or worldwide.

You can do the same for other fields of intervention, such as education, climate, customer service, personal development, etc. When crafting vision statements, keeping them short, clear, and simple is essential. A vision statement should outline an ideal yet achievable goal, setting a broad, long-term direction for your efforts. It should encapsulate where you aspire to go as a success-seeker, providing a clear and inspiring target for your endeavors. A vision statement serves as a beacon by succinctly defining your goals, guiding your actions, and uniting your stakeholders around a common goal.

Big vs. Small Vision

The vision stage in success planning defines the impact you aspire to have on others' lives and reflects your underlying motives. Are your intentions self-serving, or do they aim to benefit others? In crafting your vision statement, you can either display the breadth of your ego or demonstrate the depth of your altruism. Thinking big isn't always a sign of ego or greed; it often stems from a desire to help as many people as possible. Ultimately, a big vision means you will impact more people, benefiting the world more effectively through your endeavors. The larger the scope, the more individuals will be touched. Whether in personal or professional projects, profit or non-profit, colossal projects hold the potential to solve more problems for more people.

I am a proponent of ambitious initiatives because the process for both big and small projects remain fundamentally the same. I once met a woman at a speaking conference who shared that her successful fundraising campaign could have raised tenfold the funds if she had envisioned a bigger project. According to her, the effort wouldn't have been significantly different. The profound impact of a big vision is evident to all. Whether it's electrifying a village, city, county, or state with renewable energy, the thinking and planning process remains largely unchanged; only the scale differs.

When you think big, you inherently consider the wider community, whether consciously or not. Sometimes perceived as self-serving or greedy, this mindset can paradoxically lead to broader societal benefits, illustrating that ambition can have unexpectedly positive outcomes. This is why it's crucial to recognize that sometimes those who aim higher may achieve more, not through selfish intentions but through the sheer scale of their vision.

If you, for example, aim to build a large manufacturing plant, you can't manage it alone; you'll need a team of professionals to make it operational. I advocate for private enterprise or a free market economy because, in a world where private initiatives yield profits without negatively impacting society, thinking big pays off. The internet boom has provided striking examples of researchers, programmers, and entrepreneurs from varied backgrounds reaping substantial profits by adhering to an effective success formula. Whether crafting a personal vision statement or outlining a vision for your company or organization, the process remains consistent. Your vision sets the level of effort you intend to dedicate to a specific field, problem, or industry. Thus, you define your aspirations in terms of realizing your mission.

Fortune Cookies' Guidance: How Simple Insights Shape Our Greatest Aspirations

You might be surprised to learn that my favorite item at Chinese restaurants isn't a dish—it's the fortune cookie. Why am I so fond of fortune cookies? For several reasons. Unlike food that merely satisfies temporary hunger—and might end up on my hips—fortune cookies offer nourishment for life. They fuel our inspiration. Ideas that nourish our minds are precious, particularly when applied effectively. A single, simple idea has the potential to change your life forever.

One of my closest friends recently recounted a conversation where I had given him advice that transformed his professional life. I suggested he focus on a single profession or field of intervention rather than spreading his efforts across various fields. When he expressed his reservations, I told him English was part of his soul. Born and raised in Haiti, he mastered English in middle school. Realizing this, he developed a vision for teaching English, enabling him to excel and potentially succeed in the marketplace. To date, he has published four English teaching books aimed at helping non-native speakers. Focusing on a targeted approach, this advice dramatically increased his prospects of success as a professional or an entrepreneur.

Fortune cookies may sometimes lie to me about my personality or future, but other times, they tell the truth. Occasionally, they say something totally irrelevant. I humorously forgive the writers for not being accurate all the time because I learn from them and enjoy reading them. If you pick one occasionally, you will nourish your philosophy of life on this planet and the people around you.

I encountered a statement in one fortune cookie that deeply resonated with me: "A man's dreams are an index to his greatness." This powerful insight underscores one of the most fundamental factors influencing human success and performance. In life, those with small dreams often find themselves underperforming. Conversely, those who achieve remarkable success do so because they dream big. When fueled with passion and commitment, a dream is akin to a seed planted in fertile soil at the perfect season. Some individuals nurture monumental aspirations, continually propelling themselves to greater heights until they feel they are on the brink of touching the sky of greatness. I encourage you to dream ambitiously and diligently pursue the realization of your dream's vision. Life encompasses more than mere happiness. Innovations like airplanes, computers, artificial intelligence, and cell phones might never have been developed if humanity's goals were solely focused on joy. Instead, the ultimate goal should be to achieve success while maintaining balance, since success without balance lacks true fulfillment.

We must balance our professional and personal lives. Everyone needs time to have fun, and enjoying ourselves should not hinder our progress. Think of fun as a recess. It's not feasible to spend your entire life working; you must carve out time to rest and enjoy life. However, it's important to remember that work should take precedence over pleasure, while focusing on your primary life mission.

Dream Big for the world. Always do your best to see the big picture and think out of the box of reality and limitations. What appears immediate does not define your capacity or potential.

Dream as if there are no limits to what you can accomplish and construct a vision that can transform the field of your mission.

Crafting a Vision Statement

Being a visionary is crucial in life. This quality will help you achieve personal milestones—what we often consider succeeding in life—and enable you to fulfill your life by making a meaningful difference in the world. This broader impact gives your achievements profound significance and aligns your success with your life's purpose.

I recall the profound influence of Father Claude Chenier, who was mentioned earlier. As my religious education teacher, he introduced me to relaxation exercises and positive thinking. These early lessons led me to explore personal development tools such as philosophical yoga, affirmations, and meditation—which helped me overcome and transform life's challenges into opportunities. I am deeply thankful for his guidance, which opened doors to new paths for navigating life.

Remember, when facing challenges, you already have within you what is needed to succeed and make a difference. You possess vast capabilities; there is no human problem you cannot address. By crafting a vision that encompasses your personal goals and desires to impact others, you are setting the stage to make your life succeed through your personal and fulfilling mission, thereby achieving success with profound meaning.

You have a powerful tool you can use to build an aspirational vision for your mission—your imagination, as explained in the next section.

The Power of Your Imagination

Your imagination holds power. It enables you to inhabit a world far beyond your surroundings. At this moment, you can envision a house ten times the size of your current home. You can imagine a future filled with success and fulfilling your dreams. Your ability to conceptualize a beautification project for your city or any other major initiative is deeply rooted in your imagination. If you plan to work in a specific field, dedicate some time each day to imagine where you might be in five, ten, fifteen, or twenty years. Your imagination enables you to feel the beauty of flowers on your dream ranch, experience the thrill of your first speech in the White House or the Capitol, and celebrate your success at the Super Bowl, the Olympics, or the World Cup. It empowers you to feel the authority and power of the Fortune 500 company you are about to create or enjoy the privilege of the scholarship or business grant you deeply desire.

Imagination opens doors of opportunity, and its strength enables the realization of envisioned projects in the real world. This potent tool is at your disposal; use it daily to craft your desired life. When dissatisfied with your job or financial situation, turn to your imagination to mold your ideal circumstances. Once your vision is clear, commit it to paper as you would a vision statement. Documenting your vision lays the groundwork for turning your imaginative ideas into reality. Writing down your goals is crucial—it becomes a roadmap guiding your action plan for achieving your ideal life or project.

This reminds me of my relationship with my daughter, who complains and is often frustrated by the pens I leave scattered around the house. I always carry a pen to jot down my aspirations, the visions I aim to see materialized. Unfortunately, I sometimes leave a pen on the dining table and forget to take it back, which invariably leads to me having trouble with her. Nevertheless, I persistently document my goals using pen and paper, affirming my commitment to my dreams. I constantly use positive affirmations to transform my life and build my vision for the future through those affirmations.

Never underestimate the power of your imagination and the possibilities that your commitment can create in your life. If you allow your imagination total freedom, it will liberate you from the constraints of perceived limitations. If you believe your life is limited, it will be so. However, if you believe in your ability to create a life far better than your current one, you will imagine it and visualize all its aspects. Your imagination conditions your subconscious mind to be alert and recognize the opportunities around you. Without imagination, you cannot achieve the life you desire. Your imagination is your first ticket to the extraordinary life you dream of. Permit yourself to be bold, extravagant, and exceptional. You will create wonders and projects that improve human lives and make the world better. Let your imagination be your tool for personal growth and development.

Your imagination allows you to touch and feel the ideal life in your mind, and you must believe that you can make that vision a reality. Once you believe it, the dream will move closer to reality, and your passion will grow increasingly stronger.

Step 2 Exercises
Exercise # 1: Crafting Your Vision Statement

1. ***Discovering Your Impact***
   Consider the scope of your desired impact. Do you envision transforming the lives of individuals in your local community, or does your ambition span across towns, cities, states, or even globally? Are you focused on revolutionizing a sector by enhancing the quality of products or services, advancing an entire industry, or elevating a profession? Think about the people you aim to assist. Can you estimate the number of lives you wish to touch through your mission?

2. ***Dream Without Limits***
   Give yourself permission to dream boundlessly. Which geographic areas do you aspire to affect positively? Consider the scale of your ambition—whether you're drawn to making sweeping changes on a large scale or making a significant difference within your immediate surroundings.

3. ***Drafting Your Vision Statement***
   You're equipped to articulate a vision statement with insights from reflecting on your mission. This statement should encapsulate your core aspirations, dreams, goals, and your conception of the ideal outcome for your mission.

4. *Sample Vision Statement*

After recognizing the detrimental impact of profit-driven investors on healthcare quality in your country, you decide to champion improving healthcare services. Your vision statement could be stated as follows:

"To build a healthcare system with international standards prioritizing patient well-being through preventive care, education, and nutrition, ensuring equal access for all community members."

Please note that according to our approach, your vision statement reflects your personal mission and the goals that are deeply important to you regarding the mission's realization. You must craft this vision statement yourself; allowing others to do it for you means it won't truly represent who you are. Imitating others, especially your friends, is a significant mistake—they are on their unique paths with missions that differ from yours. Adopting someone else's perspective is comparable to trying to fit into a hat that isn't yours. Forge your own vision. Your vision statement should represent your aspirations and goals, capturing the essence of who you are and what you aim to achieve concerning your life's mission.

Exercise # 2: Creating a Mission-Focused Vision Board

1. ***What Is a Vision Board?***

   A vision board is a visual tool that embodies your aspirations, goals, and dreams. It is crafted using images, words, objects, and other elements that resonate with your vision of success and fulfillment. These components work together to represent the future you aim to realize vividly. In today's world, vision boards are either physical or digital, as mentioned in the following definition: "Vision boards are a collection of images or objects arranged to help you manifest your goals or vision. This board can be physical or digital."[28] The following is an example of a mission-focused vision board related to healthcare, with the vision of curing cancer through cancer research and professional training.

---

[28] Perry, Elizabeth. "How to Create a Vision Board." BetterUp. Accessed April 21, 2024. https://www.betterup.com/blog/how-to-create-vision-board.

6Mission-Focused Vision Board: Healthcare - Cancer Research

2. *Understanding the Difference: Mission-Focused vs. General Vision Boards*

In my research, I didn't find references to "mission-focused" vision boards, which leads me to believe I may have pioneered the concept. I developed this concept to emphasize aligning your vision board with your primary life's mission.

The key difference between mission-focused and general vision boards lies in their focus areas. While a general vision board typically encompasses a wide range of personal aspirations and desires, such as owning a luxury car or a house, a mission-focused vision board concentrates your efforts on your life's primary purpose. It is specifically crafted to reflect the impact you wish to make, the extent of your endeavors, the level of excellence you aim to achieve in your chosen field, or the transformative changes you aspire to bring about within a particular industry.

3. ***The Power of Vision Boards***
   A vision board is an effective motivational tool that keeps your goals, dreams, and aspirations in plain sight daily. Constant exposure to the visual representation of your ambitions primes your subconscious mind to align with your objectives, fostering a mindset geared towards achievement. This practice taps into the principles of the law of attraction, drawing your desires closer to reality by visualizing and manifesting the elements of your visions, objectives, and ambitions on your vision board. I constantly use the law of attraction through affirmations, both words and actions. Your mission-related vision board can help you stay focused and condition your subconscious mind to attract the elements you envision to realize your mission.

Having a sharp vision statement is essential for fulfilling your mission. As the second step in the MVP-PA model, it serves as a crucial pillar, setting the direction for your mission. With a robust vision, you move closer to your dream experience, characterized by remarkable achievements. However, developing a deep passion for your vision is vital to turn it into reality. In the next chapter, we will delve into the concept of passion as the third step in building a successful life that is both meaningful and impactful.

Chapter 6
Step 3: Find the Passion

"Nothing great in the world has ever been accomplished without passion."[29]

- Georg Wilhelm Friedrich Hegel

It is beneficial to have defined your mission and crafted a vision statement tied to that mission. Now, it's time to bring fire to the equation. Passion is the flame that cooks the meal of success. I want to share one of the stories that makes my experience as a mortgage broker unforgettable.

If you ask me, "What is the most important lesson I learned from the mortgage business?" Surprisingly, my answer is the quote mentioned above from German philosopher and writer Georg Wilhelm Friedrich Hegel.

I became a mortgage broker two months after I bought my first house in June 2003. At the time, I was making $35,000 a year and qualified for a $1,600 monthly mortgage payment.

---

[29] Georg Wilhelm Friedrich Hegel Quotes. BrainyQuote.com, BrainyMedia Inc, 2024. Accessed June 16, 2024.
https://www.brainyquote.com/quotes/georg_wilhelm_friedrich_h_101479.

The bank pre-qualified me due to my good credit. Although my credit score wasn't the highest possible, it was well above average at 693.

 Back then, a good credit score to buy a house started at an average of 620 among the three major American credit bureaus. This allowed me to secure a loan that covered the full appraised value of the house. However, my excellent credit also revealed that I needed to generate additional income to maintain house ownership. Consequently, I decided to become a mortgage broker and worked under the same mortgage broker who helped me finance my home loan. The mortgage business was very lucrative then, with banks issuing loans with fewer restrictions. Unfortunately, due to a quantity-over-quality mentality, the inevitable happened—the real estate market crashed in 2008.

I had a beneficial conversation with one of my prospects, Mr. Henry, in my office. During our discussion, we shared ideas on life events. Mr. Henry, a wood sculptor and radio host, reminded me of my dad, an excellent cabinet maker and sculptor. This connection was deepened because Mr. Henry's father was a famous sculptor from Haiti. The shared appreciation for woodcraft cemented our bond.

Mr. Henry's qualities as a radio host added another layer that motivated me to continue our conversation beyond simple business. I have a burning passion for speaking, and suddenly, the conversation was no longer just about business. Life, after all, is more important than the commissions I earn from writing a mortgage loan. During our discussion, Mr. Henry mentioned a powerful quote by Georg Wilhelm Friedrich Hegel. Since that day, the quote has resonated with me.

I learned and memorized this short quote, which everyone should know by heart: "Nothing great in the world has been accomplished without passion." Understanding that my mission is to speak and write to improve lives, and recognizing this as a sacred truth for personal growth, I retained this quote of wisdom to share with the world in an impactful way. In my quest for answers, I realized that the third step on the road to achievement is to find passion for our mission.

As Hegel said, without passion, our realizations will lack greatness. Passion truly makes us powerful beyond measure. At the end of this chapter, we aim for you to write an inspiring passion statement for your mission that can fuel your motivation for the excellent execution of your life's plan.

7 Passion: The Flame of Motivation for Big Achievements

The Power of Passion

Passion ignites an unwavering zeal for your dreams, missions, plans, and aspirations, propelling you toward unparalleled heights of achievement and fulfillment. When fueled by passion, your actions carry the power of realization. While some may interchange the words mission and passion in sentences, it's essential to recognize that mission directs the course of your life, while passion fuels the why behind it. It electrifies your mission and represents the intensity of your commitment to your dreams, plans, and life projects.

Passion remains crucial because, as Hegel reminded us, we cannot accomplish anything of terrific value without it.

Hegel bestowed upon us one of humanity's most profound lessons. Allow me to extend an invitation to explore the significant worth and boundless power of passion within these pages. I encourage you to contemplate your passion's transformative influence on your mission. Just as we did for dreams, passion deserves to be described poetically.

Passion: The Heartbeat of Achievement

Passion is fire.

Passion is energy.

Passion is love.

Passion is electricity.

Passion is light.

Passion is power.

Passion is excitement.

Passion remains the highest level of motivation.

Passion builds faith.

Passion creates momentum.

Passion brings persistence and determination.

Passion cements your life dreams and mission.

Passion will make you feel invincible.

Passion strengthens your imagination and helps you visualize unimaginable possibilities.

Passion gives discipline.

Passion solidifies your resolution.

Passion is critical in building lasting success.

Passion eliminates obstacles.

Passion fuels the power behind the law of attraction.

With passion, you will attract what you want.

Passion creates champions.

Passion builds stars.

Passion makes MVPs (Most Valuable Players).

Passion produces leaders.

Passion brings victory and triumph.

Passion is strength.

Passion is your ticket to success.

Passion will take you to the finish line.

Passion overcomes procrastination.

Passion breeds winners.

With your passion, the sky of achievement is reachable because it will propel you to a prominent level of your potential. The great empires are built with a bold vision, but without the passion for that vision, those great empires would never have existed.

When there is passion, you will find the resources. Consider going out for lunch with a friend. If you are passionate about the friendship, your brain becomes primed to retain all the information your friend shares with you. You prioritize time for the relationship. Conversely, without passion, you will likely forget most of the information your friend shared during your time together.

Passion can be likened to a food spice. As someone from the Caribbean, I know the value of spice. Passion does for success what a spice does for a meal. A tasteless meal can be elevated with just a touch of spice. To achieve remarkable success, it's crucial to discover the formula of passion for your mission.

Your passion will lead you to say "No" when everyone expects a "Yes." When a request does not align with your passion, the best response is often "No." Saying "No" is not impolite; it simply means the request does not match what you are passionate about.

Passion will take you to the peak of success and greatness through resilience and determination. Passion is comparable to the fire that ignites your action plan, providing the intensity needed to make you shine like the morning star. Without passion, you risk being average in your profession, business, scientific pursuits, or inventions. It is the driving force behind all MVPs and is a constant element in all champions.

My Total Body Transformation: A Great Story of Passion

I refer to this stage in the journey toward success as the justification phase. In project management, a specific phase is known as justification, which is particularly evident when drafting a funding proposal. This proposal section aims to demonstrate why the project is essential to the funding partner. It's where you uncover the reasons to persuade yourself and your stakeholders that you're on the right path. Just as the justification section is crucial in project management, passion holds equal importance in achieving success. You must be capable of justifying to yourself why you are pursuing your mission's goals, and these reasons must be compelling.

In 2019, some of my former high school classmates formed a WhatsApp group to organize a boot camp in Florida for the first quarter of 2020 to help members stay in good shape. I committed myself to this project because I knew it would help me stay healthy, and it has been incredibly beneficial to me. My level of dedication was evident; after attending the boot camp on the first Saturday of the movement, I went to my community park and walked an additional four miles to further progress toward my goals. Every morning since then, I spend at least 15 minutes exercising in front of my mirror and constantly weigh myself to track my progress. Sometimes, I even exercised after waking up at night to use the bathroom, all in pursuit of progress.

During a visit to New York to see my dad at my sister's house, I enlisted my nephew as my unpaid coach for the week, asking him to teach me techniques to achieve my goal of six-pack abs. He gladly took me to his gym in Brooklyn, where he taught me various exercises and recommended dietary habits to help me reach my goals. We captured some of these moments on video and shared them with the group chat, including footage of me exercising in my tie. Though I may have seemed crazy, I was exercising my passion towards achieving my fitness goals.

I stayed motivated by sharing my personal goals with the group and seeking advice from classmates who have succeeded in the fitness arena. These steps reflect my motivation level toward making my goals a reality. This passion is essential for success. You must cultivate an unparalleled passion for your mission's primary goals to succeed.

In the next section, we will attempt to discover the fundamental components of passion, which demonstrate how to recognize passion for a mission or project.

Components of Passion

Passion is essential for personal growth and success, serving as the binding agent in your endeavors. For any project to excel, it requires a significant amount of passion. Reflecting on Hegel's thoughts about passion, I often remind myself that lacking passion for a job or industry likely means success will be unattainable there. While some may decide to persevere until passion is discovered, genuine passion frequently begins as an inner voice guiding one toward a specific event or organization, even if profound enthusiasm isn't immediately evident. Passion is critical as it acts as a foundational support for your primary goals. To identify and nurture this passion, ask yourself the following questions:

- Can I persevere through the toughest challenges?
- Will I keep going even if opposed or discouraged by others?
- What are my limits in facing challenges and seizing opportunities?
- How resolute am I, and can I prioritize my goals over others?

Addressing these questions will determine whether investing your efforts in this path is worthwhile. When your passion is aligned with your purpose, it enhances your motivation, self-discipline, commitment, and focus, driving your project or mission forward. Let's explore these components individually.

1. Motivation

Motivation for the job at hand is a quality highly valued by all employers. Job postings often specify the need for someone who is self-motivated, which sets high and challenging expectations. While technical skills can be taught, true motivation must come from within. This inherent quality is difficult for managers to instill, which is why I recommend that recruiters and managers avoid rushing hiring decisions. I prefer maintaining staff on temporary status rather than committing to employees who lack motivation and may challenge leadership and management throughout their tenure.

As a father, I actively encourage my children to engage in activities or choose careers that ignite their personal motivation. For you to find your path, you should explore essential questions such as:

- *What's my why?*

- *Am I connected to a higher purpose?*

- *What impact can I make individually?*

Passion drives motivation, and motivation can likewise spark further passion. Realizing one's true purpose on this planet and connecting life to a higher goal—whether it's achieving personal success, addressing significant global challenges, or influencing future generations—can lead to profound motivation.

It is possible for individuals to be motivated by the pursuit of specific achievements yet lack deep passion. While this can temporarily sustain motivation, genuine passion inspires and catalyzes meaningful change. Possessing all

the academic credentials or even Albert Einstein's intellect is less meaningful without deep, personal motivation. Without it, all skills and qualities risk being underutilized.

2. *Self-Discipline*

In chapter three, we explored the invaluable concept of personal responsibility and displayed self-discipline as an essential part. Passion is also expressed through self-discipline. As we have mentioned, passion can be everything, as it is the flame that keeps all the steps interconnected. In this section, we consider another definition from the Collins dictionary, which describes discipline as "the ability to control yourself and to make yourself work hard or behave in a particular way without needing anyone else to tell you what to do."[30] This definition encapsulates what I aim to achieve in exploring the concept of passion. Self-discipline is demonstrated through controlled behavior and adherence to established rules and standards without pressure. To achieve your goals, you must act in accordance with established guidelines without any influence from external forces.

---

[30] Self-discipline," s.v. *Collins English Dictionary*, accessed April 23, 2024, https://www.collinsdictionary.com/dictionary/english/self-discipline.

Passion is expressed through self-discipline. Passion will give you the discipline you need to learn the rules of your industry and adhere to them, especially if you aspire to be an integral part of your organization or excel in your profession. Knowing these rules is crucial. A student enthusiastic about achieving superior results, for example, applies self-discipline at school and home to succeed. They understand that lacking discipline makes it more challenging to pass final exams. This type of behavior is applied to any situation where the individual nurtures a passion for a particular goal or activity.

With the appropriate level of passion, you will cultivate robust discipline. This discipline enables you to decline invitations that conflict with your priorities, such as choosing to study for an exam when friends ask you to go out. Self-discipline is also essential in professional settings—ensuring you wake up at a specific time to manage appointments or open your business on time requires setting a precise bedtime. When working on a project, you won't pursue new ventures unless your schedule allows. Ultimately, you adhere strictly to the rules of your field or those set by your organization.

3. *Commitment*

Commitment is essential in fueling your passion for a project or mission. Consider the example of a relationship: if one partner is unwilling to commit, the future of the relationship is uncertain, signaling a lack of serious intent. Similarly, a lack of commitment in any endeavor suggests a low level of passion. When true passion exists, you naturally dedicate time and resources. This is evident when someone deeply in love invests significantly in their relationship, demonstrating a strong mix of commitment and passion.

In professional or personal projects, commitment is evidenced by tangible allocations of resources, such as time, money, and effort. Without these, it is difficult to justify or encourage investment in the project. Setting goals without a robust commitment to seeing them through will likely lead to disappointment and frustration, resulting from wasted time and resources.

4. *Focus*

Focus is a crucial component of passion. When passion is present, focus naturally follows. True passion is expressed through unwavering focus on your primary mission or goal. Merriam-Webster defines focus as "directed attention, emphasis,"[31] a definition perfectly aligned with our objective for this section. We want you to view focus as your ability to concentrate your attention on a singular goal, giving it your full dedication.

Focusing on a primary goal makes you more efficient with your time, attention, and resources. I vividly recall a decision I made when presented with an opportunity in the insurance business. I made the conscious choice to divert my attention from other potential ventures, such as real

---

[31] Focus," s.v. *Merriam-Webster.com Dictionary*. Accessed April 23, 2024. https://www.merriam-webster.com/dictionary/focus.

estate, home financing, and technical support. Instead, I resolved to channel all my efforts into the insurance business to ensure my success in the field. In effect, the success has been remarkable. I recognize that sign of success in people when they focus on a unique goal or mission. By maintaining focus on your mission, you can confidently pursue your vision until it becomes a reality.

In the next section, I will introduce a powerful tool at your disposal to build passion for your primary life mission. If you utilize this tool effectively, you will gain the necessary components of passion you need to advance the primary cause of your life.

Affirmations and Passion Building

I have several personal stories I could share with you about this powerful tool you use every day: your words. You should consider everything you say to be affirmations and be mindful of what you repeat daily. If you want something, then repeat it over and over. I recommend having special affirmation sessions two or three times a day to build your confidence around your goals.

Personally, I have been using affirmations for over thirty-five years and in diverse types of settings. I have diaries that I use to write my affirmations. If you have a chance to visit my diaries, you will see that many of these affirmations have become reality. That's a technique they have used in certain schools to help students build healthy habits. For example, if you are constantly late coming to school, they make you write "I will come to school on time every day" one thousand times. This is the technique of affirmation in practice. The student will internalize the principle by affirming the statement repetitively until it becomes true.

In our context, you must deliberately choose to transform your life and use affirmations to get you there. Affirmations must always be written in a positive format. In disciplines that practice affirmations as an achievement-building tool, the subconscious mind is believed not to process negative statements effectively. Therefore, focusing on positive outcomes is generally recommended. As a practitioner, I understand that if I say, "Do not smoke," the subconscious mind may only pick up the word "smoke." Therefore, it is more effective to use positive affirmations. For instance, a smoker who wants to quit should affirm, "I am breathing fresh air and taking good care of my lungs every day," to focus on the desired outcome and reinforce positive behavior.

In the Catholic religion, people use the rosary to pray and repeat the same prayer multiple times. This technique of repetition can also be adapted to repeat your affirmations. In various Eastern religions, similar techniques are used to achieve the same goal: making wishes or dreams come true. While affirmations are often considered to be just words, I define an affirmation as anything you do to reinforce your beliefs about something. This aligns with the popular motivational phrase 'fake it till you make it,' emphasizing the power of belief and consistent practice in achieving your goals.

I remember my college days in Haiti vividly. Every month, my dad would send me money from Brooklyn, NY. Whenever it arrived, I'd treat myself to dinner at a fancy restaurant in Pétion-Ville, a city known for its affluent residents. These meals were more than just extravagances; they were a bold declaration of the prosperity I was determined to achieve one day. I usually tipped the server more than average, as if I were a wealthy man, affirming my wealth through my actions.

You should use all the tools at your disposal to match your subconscious mind to the dreams that you nurture. If you affirm, "I am wealthy," but simultaneously hold tightly to your money, your subconscious mind may struggle to align with this wealthy self-image. This discrepancy can hinder truly embracing a rich person's mindset. Once your belief system is firmly established, your actions become the most effective tools in turning your dreams into reality.

If someone wants to make an impact in education as an innovator, they can use the following affirmation:

"I am the source of innovation for the education system in America. I am convinced that I will generate solutions to improve the system, helping the children of this country receive an education focused on critical thinking, positive psychology, and creativity."

The next section introduces supportive networks as another way to create passion for achievement.

Building Passion with Positive Reinforcement: The Power of Supportive Networks

I was born in the countryside of Haiti. My parents probably took me to Port-au-Prince, the capital city, at the age of five. I went to school at six, which was a little late compared to most middle-class children. Because my academic results were satisfactory, my dad had me skip two grades when they enrolled me in my first public school. However, that school experience turned out to be disappointing. I felt disconnected and was stuck in the same grade for two years; the support system was almost nonexistent. Additionally, the school environment was strained by overcrowded classrooms and insufficient teacher attention. I could not manage to earn good grades, and my parents blamed me, assuming I prioritized play over study.

Due to a lack of support and positive reinforcement, I struggled to meet the expected performance standards, even though my dad, confident in my abilities, had me skip two grades. The specifics of his arrangement remain unclear to me. He is a person of action—meaningfully successful and decisive, always stepping in whenever necessary.

After enduring two years of setbacks, my dad truly embodied the principle of "father knows best." He successfully transferred me to a smaller public school in our neighborhood. Although I did not pass, my dad somehow managed to advance me to the next grade. Don't ask me how he accomplished that, but he did it once again.

In 1978, I embarked on a special phase of my educational journey at a local public elementary school, "Ecole Nationale Hermann Heraux." During this time, I encountered one of the most unforgettable moments of my life. During a regular class session, Mrs. Caleus, the school dean, made a special effort to interrupt her meeting in another classroom just to come and listen as I eloquently read a text to my classmates under the supervision of my teacher.

Wow! I knew I had done well! From that day on, Mrs. Caleus took me under her wing, constantly encouraging me and showing her belief in my abilities and her affection for me. She even advised my mother not to let me eat at neighbors' houses to prevent potential harm. From that day forward, I led the school by topping my class nearly every quarter. I became a well-known and beloved student. Everyone knew through the publicity from the school staff that I was a bright child. One noteworthy event was that I was allowed to eat for free in the school cafeteria, thanks to my good grades. Mrs. Caleus remains an unforgettable figure in my life—she instilled a passion for success in me. She should be proud of the impact she had on my life. She is the kind of educator every parent hopes their children will have. It is worth noting that many older individuals and role models in my neighborhood also supported me incredibly.

I caught the vibe, and I built a passion for success. I received the support I needed to succeed as a student at École Nationale Hermann Heraux (Public Elementary School in Port-au-Prince, Haiti). This school provided me with the foundation necessary to build a successful career. After elementary school, I moved to a Catholic school, where I found another strong support system fostered by many classmates and teachers.

When you surround yourself with people who consistently show their belief in you, you gain the ability to excel. Avoiding negative influences creates opportunities to use your talents and achieve extraordinary things. Stay away from those who never see a path to success, even your family members. Block out suggestions filled with vibes of limitations. Do not let them paralyze the MVP within you.

Choose friends, coworkers, and neighbors who can help you cultivate a success mindset. Maintain contact with people who would act just like Mrs. Caleus did in my life: always ready to push me to do my best by showing her belief in my potential.

If they cannot offer you positive support, you should stop sharing your ideas with them. Negative people can damage your productivity and, most importantly, your creativity. They are not only dream killers but also creativity stiflers. Negative individuals hinder your ability to generate innovative ideas, design solutions for your problems, and annihilate your efficiency. Conversely, positive individuals like Mrs. Caleus help you become more productive and creative by encouraging your brain to generate fresh solutions and ideas. They enhance your thinking ability, resulting in better productivity and creativity. When people expect you to succeed, you are more likely to surprise the world with superior performances or outcomes. Indeed, positive expectations can positively impact your results. Always surround yourself with positive people—those who believe in you, as Mrs. Caleus believed in her students and expected them to succeed.

It is also important to surround yourself with productive people. If you seek success, look for individuals who share your goals. Target people who aspire to advance and find ways to connect with them. Build connections with individuals who are enthusiastic about success and fulfillment. Friends and connections can often influence the scope of your aspirations and the magnitude of your achievements.

You can achieve greatness. All you need is a welcoming environment of supportive people who can awaken the passion for success within you. Building a support group for your mission's aspirations will foster an empowering passion for outstanding performance. Positive reinforcement and encouragement undoubtedly help cultivate passion for success.

Your quest for achievement is essential for the world; many people depend on it, and there are people who naturally want to help you achieve your mission. That's why the next section emphasizes that quitting is not an option.

Quitting Is Not an Option

Perseverance remains a remarkable quality for individuals driven by passion. Passion provides the strength needed to endure until the battle's end. You are like a soldier marching into war to defend their country. Knowing that the freedom or welfare of the nation rests on their shoulders, their determination to emerge victorious is unwavering.

The pursuit of success can be likened to a never-ending battle. Life thrives on new challenges; without them, it can become routine. Challenges are inherent, urging you to take risks and confront new obstacles continually. Therefore, it's imperative to adopt a mindset that refuses surrender. Victory becomes the only option. Your life transforms into a priceless asset for all those who rely on your success.

Only an elevated level of passion can guarantee the kind of determination that will keep you alert and robust in continuing the fight. Life is not a struggle for winners; instead, it is a battle that demands arduous work to win the war and achieve victory. Success is not reserved for those who believe life should be easy and filled with constant fun. While happiness is vital, aiming solely for happiness is insufficient. Success in your mission, with its impact on others' lives, demands hard work and constant dedication to be a priority on your agenda.

Many systems promote a life of immense success with minimal effort, preaching wealth without exertion—America has plenty of these get-rich-quick scams. However, success cannot be attained through intelligence alone. You must invest time, exercise patience, and put in the effort required to reach the light at the end of the success tunnel.

Success results from unequivocal perseverance. While working smart can lead to greatness, it alone cannot transform your long-term mission into concrete results. Remarkable success, without a doubt, demands time, resources, and energy investment.

Failures are an inevitable part of life; it's not just about triumphs. Anyone who suggests otherwise is not being truthful. However, they can assure you that things will be all right if you persevere and don't give up halfway. Along the way, expect to face some defeats. Don't begin with the expectation that everything will be perfect.

Your passion remains the driving force that can carry you through the challenges you will face. Therefore, it is crucial to cultivate an immense amount of passion around your mission to sustain your journey. All types of obstacles will block your way. Sometimes, you may be inclined to decline requests for more investments, more time, or more courage. Only your passion will rescue you in such moments and propel you towards realization.

The level of stress generated by the mission can affect your health and family life. You may even lose friends along the way, and your environment could become negative. However, your passion can serve as a source of strength and support in such challenging times.

The term passion is not new, but the MVP-PA system makes it integral to a success model. The new concept introduced in personal development is called a passion statement. The next section will show my passion statement and explain the concept.

My Passion Statement and Explanation of the Concept

My Passion Statement

I have chosen to communicate to improve people's lives because, at age eleven, I discovered my vocation and passion for speaking to inspire change. I love speaking, and I thrive in front of crowds. I am electrified whenever I have the opportunity to address an audience. I am convinced that my mission is to improve people's lives by sharing messages of hope, faith, success, and happiness.

Since discovering my vocation and passion for speaking, I have dedicated my life to speaking to improve people's lives. At the Catholic chapel of my dad's home village, I was, during summer vacations, a young preacher who motivated people to embrace change and work to become better individuals. In 1990, as a member of a yoga center, the director chose me to lead the Wednesday class. Every Sunday, I was one of several center members standing before the audience, reading our affirmations aloud and having the group repeat them. In primary and middle school, teachers selected me to read dictations to the class. My voice and intonation became my assets as a student and a member of any organization.

At 16, I wrote my first poem, "Adonis." Adonis was a character I created—a youngster to whom I advised, through the poem, on how to behave to lead a balanced life and succeed. Furthermore, when I embraced painting after high school as a hobby and an eventual addition to my professional career, I created paintings intended to enhance the individual human experience. Speaking, writing, and art are the vehicles

I use to make a difference in people's lives. Moreover, I prioritize behaving and acting in ways that inspire those around me toward success and progress.

I enjoy speaking for change, personal development, education, peace, love, progress, personal responsibility, success, wisdom, and humility. I aspire for my voice, art, writings, and actions to serve as vehicles for personal development and achievement.

Therefore, I am committed to enhancing the individual human experience through personal development by communicating through speaking, writing, and painting. This last statement shows that improving the individual human experience through personal development is my mission, and I use my vocations of communication and art to carry it out.

The Why of My Mission

The reason behind my mission is deeply rooted in my personal experiences and the profound impact that communication has had on my life. From an early age, I realized that my voice had the power to influence and inspire others. This realization fueled my passion and solidified my commitment to using my communication skills to bring about positive change.

I have witnessed the transformative power of words through various stages of my life, whether in church, school, or social settings. My mission is driven by the desire to share this gift with others, to help them find hope, faith, success, and happiness. By communicating my uplifting messages effectively, I can contribute to a better world where individuals are empowered to reach their full potential.

The Concept of a Passion Statement

In project management, there is a concept called project justification, which provides a clear rationale for undertaking a project. I have imported this concept into personal development, coining the term "passion statement." While personal development literature often encourages individuals to find their passion, it has not typically used the term "passion statement." Mission and vision statements in business management articulate a company's purpose and aspirations.

The passion statement adds an additional step in the personal development process: mission statement (1), vision statement (2), and passion statement (3). The justification section should add more value to the mission and vision statements. You answer clearly why you have made these choices, making it easy for stakeholders to understand the direction and purpose of the company, the project, and, in our context, your direction, purpose, and mission.

The passion statement helps strengthen the commitment to the mission and vision statements. It goes beyond merely identifying one's passion; it formalizes it into a statement that provides direction and motivation. This structured approach helps individuals align their actions with their core values and goals, similar to how mission and vision statements and a clear justification of those statements guide a business. Individuals can gain clarity and focus by articulating a passion statement, enhancing their personal development journey.

With your written statements of mission, vision, and passion, you have built the foundational steps of your life's success. The final two chapters will cover personal life planning and action, equipping you with the necessary tools to perfect the success recipe.

Step 3 Exercise

Write a Passion Statement for Your Mission.

Follow these steps to articulate why your mission is significant to you.

1. ***Reflect on Your Core Values***
   List your most important values. How do these values drive your mission?

2. ***Identify Critical Needs***
   Consider the needs of the population you aim to serve. How does your mission address these specific problems?

3. ***Draw from Personal Experience***
   Think about personal stories or pivotal moments that have shaped your life. How do these experiences inspire your dedication?

4. ***Write Your Statement***
   Combine your values, the needs you aim to meet, and your inspiration into a concise statement that captures the essence of your mission and justifies why you have chosen your vision.

Remember, your Passion Statement should resonate deeply with your motivations and aspirations. Use it to remind yourself of the deeper reasons behind your daily actions and long-term goals.

Chapter 7
Step 4: Build a Mission-Focused Personal Plan

"You were born to win, but to be a winner, you must plan to win, prepare to win, and expect to win."[32]

– Zig Ziglar

Not having a plan leaves success to chance. While nurturing a great vision is crucial, it alone isn't sufficient. A detailed plan is necessary to turn that vision into reality. Although I previously emphasized having a mission, vision, and passion, I consider these steps as parts of the dream aspect of success. This chapter will delve into the practical details of what makes people successful in accomplishing their missions. This is no longer about dreaming; this is the stage where we clearly

understand the resources at our disposal, the time we can allocate, the people we need, and what we need to

---

[32] Zig Ziglar Quotes. BrainyQuote.com, BrainyMedia Inc, 2024. https://www.brainyquote.com/quotes/zig_ziglar_381983, accessed April 24, 2024.

communicate to our stakeholders. We set clear and smart goals and objectives, developing strategies and tactics needed to turn our life's mission into reality. Just like a house needs a solid foundation, so does your life. The process of building your mission, vision, and passion remains the foundation of your life's project. This forms the basis of your MVP status in life. With a clear mission, a solid vision, and a strong passion for success, you are equipped to succeed and lead a fulfilled life. With this solid foundation, you are ready to become one of the MVPs or champions of this planet.

8Plan: The Roadmap for Execution

A plan is a tool that outlines your choices about how to use the resources available to you. Saying someone has a plan implies that they know where they have made specific decisions on utilizing their resources. Now is the time to use your brain and imagination to build a solid set of directions for your life. If you make intelligent choices, you can turn your dreams into reality and share your success with the world.

Conducting market research is crucial when writing a business plan. These research results serve as the plan's guiding compass, allowing you to understand market trends, customer habits and preferences, competition, and supply availability. Similarly, knowing yourself and understanding your marketplace are essential to personal growth. Self-awareness and marketplace insight are vitally important.

The Magic of Simplification

A plan allows you to divide a big problem into small pieces that are easier to manage. When all small pieces are fixed, the problem as a whole will be resolved, or small solutions can be synchronized to resolve the big issue. That's what we do when we divide a task into several parts. When we want to solve a country's problem, we divide the country into states, provinces, or departments. When we need to solve a state's problems, we divide the state into counties. When we want to solve the problems of a county, we divide the county into cities, and so on. This process occurs in every learning project, class, or program. A learning project may have distinct parts, but the best way to impart knowledge is to divide it into different classes or units until you complete the whole program. By dissecting a problem or project to identify all the necessary parts, you gain the ability to understand the big picture and propose effective solutions or execute projects efficiently.

Breaking down a complex issue into smaller, manageable pieces facilitates resolution. This approach is evident in various contexts, such as dividing tasks among teams, addressing national issues by dividing countries into states or provinces, and solving local problems by dividing regions into counties and cities. Simplifying complex problems enables us to tackle them more effectively and efficiently.

Personal SWOT Analysis (Self-Awareness)

In the business world, a SWOT [33] analysis provides organizations with a clear picture of their Strengths, Weaknesses, Opportunities, and Threats, aiding them in navigating the marketplace successfully. Similarly, a personal SWOT analysis offers an invaluable framework for understanding your unique position in various contexts—your career, personal life, or other endeavors. By dividing the analysis into four distinct sections—Strengths, Weaknesses, Opportunities, and Threats—you gain deep insights into your personal capabilities and challenges.

Notice that this analytical tool is not just about identifying what you are good at or what challenges you face; it's about recognizing how you can leverage your strengths to take advantage of opportunities and how you can manage or mitigate your weaknesses to avoid potential pitfalls. The following are items you can consider in each of the four sections of your personal SWOT analysis:

Strengths (Internal, Positive Aspects)

- Skills
- Personality Traits
- Training and Education
- Credentials
- Financial Position

---

[33] Albert S. Humphrey, *SWOT Analysis* (Stanford Research Institute, 1970).

- Relationships
- Conflict Resolution
- Creativity
- Positive Attitude
- Support System
- Intelligence Quotient (IQ)
- Emotional Intelligence (EI)
- Contacts
- Professional Outlook

Weaknesses (Internal, Negative Aspects)

- Lack of Certain Transferable Skills
- Personality Traits Impacting Relationships and Performance
- Need for Professional Improvement
- Limited Contacts
- Lack of Focus
- Conflict Mishandling
- Resource Constraints
- Health Challenges
- Anxiety
- Lack of Motivation
- Stress Mishandling

Opportunities (External, Positive Aspects)

- Market Trends
- Funding Opportunities and Available Grants

- Consumer Behavior Tendencies
- Marketplace Needs
- Technological Advancements
- Artificial Intelligence
- Social Media Opportunities
- Regulatory Changes
- Demographic Shifts
- Networking Events and Professional Associations
- Globalization
- Personal Development Programs
- Access to Information and Training

Threats (External, Negative Aspects)

- Inflation
- Increase in Labor Costs
- Global Conflicts
- Political Crises
- Hate Crimes
- Neighborhood Issues
- Workforce Shortages
- Mass Shootings
- Environmental Issues
- Price Fluctuations
- Family Interferences
- Social Disturbances

A well-articulated SWOT analysis enables you to determine areas to strengthen your position. It helps you identify and capitalize on opportunities, understand how to mitigate threats, and strategically address weaknesses that may impede progress in achieving your mission. By systematically evaluating these four aspects—Strengths, Weaknesses, Opportunities, and Threats—you can develop a more focused and effective strategy for reaching your goals. This process reveals your current standing and charts a realistic and actionable path forward. To maximize the benefits of a SWOT analysis, consider asking yourself specific questions such as: How can I leverage my strengths to capitalize on identified opportunities? What strategies can I implement to address my weaknesses? How should I respond to external threats that may impact my mission?

Goal Setting

The cornerstone of any plan or project proposal is the main goal the entrepreneur or organization's founder strives to achieve. Every activity, strategy, and tactic outlined in the plan directly supports this main goal, clarifying what needs to be accomplished to realize your vision. While your vision may be idealistic, your goal should aim for something tangible, concrete, and measurable.

I want to introduce a concept often used in goal setting: SMART goals[34]. The acronym SMART stands for:

S: Specific
The goal must be <u>specific</u>, clearly defining who, what, why, where, which, and when.

M: Measurable
The goal needs to be <u>measurable</u>. When the goal is defined correctly, it is easier to establish criteria for measuring progress towards its realization.

A: Achievable
<u>Achievable</u> means the goal should be realistic and attainable within your capabilities and constraints. However, in personal development, we should approach "achievable" with flexibility, as one can

---

[34] George T. Doran, "There's a S.M.A.R.T. Way to Write Management's Goals and Objectives," *Management Review* 70, no. 11 (1981): 35-36.

never truly imagine the extent of one's potential when one's passion for a goal becomes boundless.

R: Relevant
The goal should matter to you and align with the other significant goals in your life project or plan.

T: Time-bound
A real goal has a deadline or a timeframe for achievement. It will help if you consider it as not having one until you set a deadline or timeframe to achieve your goal.

This means that goals should be specific, measurable, achievable, relevant, and time-bound. SMART goals are commonly utilized in management and are recommended in personal development for their benefits. I want to emphasize that you should feel empowered when setting your mission's goals. Try not to restrict your ambitions. If you are committed to your goal, you can achieve it. Your passion and persistence will help you reach the peak of the mountain.

In summary, your life goals should be deeply rooted in your mission and need to be SMART and bold.

What is the main goal you wish to achieve to feel that you have fulfilled your mission? Establishing a focused, mission-driven personal plan is essential for this purpose. Additionally, I would like to briefly discuss the importance of a personal development plan designed to enhance your chances of success. Creating a personal development plan will give you direction and aid in effectively accomplishing your mission.

Do You Have a Mission-Focused Personal Plan?

A personal plan breaks down your life project into distinct parts; each systematically addressed to achieve your important life goals. Similarly, a business plan clearly outlines the aims of a business, project, or organization, typically consisting of three main parts: marketing, operational, and financial plans.

 Focusing on a communication plan, a financial plan, and an action plan is advisable for your personal mission.

A comprehensive plan answers six fundamental questions—who, what, when, where, why, and how—using a model known as the 5W1H[35]This model simplifies the planning process and facilitates effective execution. Remember, while your plan doesn't need to detail every aspect exhaustively, it should cover all the essentials.

The primary function of a plan is to provide you with a clear roadmap that leads to the execution of your project. It helps visualize the big picture and understand the different elements necessary to materialize your vision of success. Having a clear plan is crucial to reaching your mission's goals.

In planning, remember that understanding the landscape of opportunities is vital. More people are willing to help than you might realize, along with ample government funding and

---

[35] Five Ws and One H: The 5W1H Approach." Continuous Improvement Toolkit. Accessed June 19, 2024. https://citoolkit.com/articles/five-ws/

volunteers waiting for your invitation. Sometimes, a friend or a family member might possess the needed resources, but your preconceived notions about their capabilities could blind you to these potential contributions.

When planning, envision a world full of potential. The true winners are those who maintain a positive outlook and see endless possibilities. Throughout my career as an insurance agent, I have encountered many successful people who attribute their success to their positivity and ability to see the world as infinite possibilities. Great hope produces bold actions and, therefore, impressive results.

Your mission-focused personal plan must answer some key questions: What are your financial needs and current financial situation? How will you communicate with your target audience and market your personal project? What action steps are needed to materialize the vision? Everything must align with the goal, and every action you take must align with it.

Setting a clear goal allows you to be specific and make precise choices regarding what you want to accomplish to turn your mission into reality. Consider this example of a specific goal for a mission focused on education: "To build a not-for-profit high school in Los Angeles, providing access to approximately 5000 underprivileged students by October 1st, 2025."

By clearly specifying your goals related to your mission, you ensure that every step taken is purposeful and directed toward achieving your vision.

The Personal Development Plan

A personal development plan will set you apart. The following sections are intended to guide you in planning your personal growth as a professional or an entrepreneur, ensuring a smooth execution of your success and mission. Figure 9 elegantly illustrates the different sections of the plan.

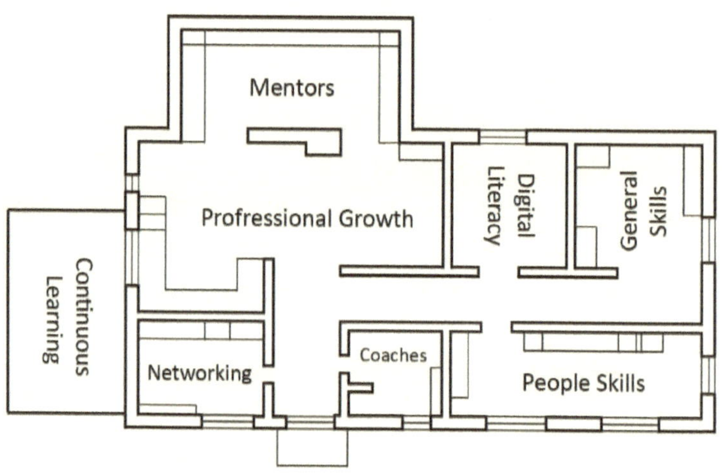

9Personal Development Plan: What do You Need to Take Your Life to the Next Level?

1. Professional Growth and Continuous Learning

As a professional, you should possess a level of expertise in a profession or trade that makes you highly sought after in the marketplace. Learning must be a continuous process throughout your life; never assume you have finished learning. The chapter on personal responsibility highlights continuous self-improvement as a crucial component. Both you and your organization must evolve in a constantly changing environment. Without ongoing learning, your competitors will outpace you by innovating with new products or services.

Remember, your profession always evolves, so continuing education is essential across various industries. Always strive to stay updated with your field's latest techniques and ideas. By continually learning, you ensure that your customers and employers can rely on your advice and solutions when needed.

Identifying the areas you need to master to realize your vision is critical. Fulfilling learning requirements does not necessarily require a college degree; your needs will depend on your current knowledge and your goals. The broader your vision, the more learning it necessitates. It's admirable that in America, you can attend a short course, pass a state exam, and obtain a license or certification that may offer financial benefits comparable to or better than those holding a college degree. College degrees are important, but they are not suited for everyone. Society equally needs trade professionals and those with academic degrees. There is room for every skill set.

The key is a commitment to continuous learning and improvement, which will safeguard not only your position and your company but also your industry, thereby contributing to the country's advancement.

2. *People Skills Development*

My professor conducted an enlightening exercise worth sharing in my interpersonal communication class at Edmonds Community College in Lynnwood, Washington. He asked everyone to hurl insulting words at him to demonstrate how to remain composed and not get upset by others' words. Often, we react negatively without understanding the other person's intent.

The teacher emphasized the importance of conducting a perception check during conversations in this class. This is crucial because many interpersonal conflicts arise simply from misunderstandings between the parties involved.

I encourage you to explore the concept of emotional intelligence as part of your journey toward success. Some individuals fail to reach top positions not because of a lack of skills, but because of a lack of emotional intelligence, despite being highly suitable for those promotions. People skills can be considered general or transferable; therefore, they are useful in all professional settings. Although there is a subsection titled General Skills Development, emphasizing people skills separately is critical.

3. *Selecting a Mentor*

Plan to have mentors throughout your career, but consider finding a new mentor each time you start a new position, launch a business, or join a new organization. My early days as an insurance sales agent at Humana were challenging. Despite holding an MBA, I quickly learned that anyone with a high school diploma could succeed in this industry. Moreover, I was tasked with targeting a primarily uneducated and low-income segment of the market, which required interacting with people from diverse ethnic backgrounds—adding another layer of complexity to my role.

During a particularly discouraging phase, I sought advice from a manager named Franz Lorenz, who shared the wisdom he had gleaned from the Bible. Franz recounted a lesson from Paul the Apostle, who said, 'I have become all things to all people, that I might save some.'[36] This meant that Paul, as a communicator and preacher, adapted his approach to resonate with the diverse people he encountered, thereby facilitating more effective communication and, ultimately, their conversion to his teachings.

Franz's advice was transformative for me. It revealed a trade secret that proved particularly useful during my one-on-one meetings with prospects. Inspired by this, I

---

[36] 1 Corinthians 9:22, New International Version.

embraced local customs when visiting people's homes—
whether it was sharing a cup of coffee, dining with them,
mingling with prospects, or engaging in respectful,
lighthearted humor. This adaptability significantly
contributed to my success as a sales agent.

4. *Partnering with a Coach*

Authoring this book -*Success with Meaning*- has been
instrumental in highlighting the importance of partnering
with a coach in our personal lives. I had been planning to
write it for almost five years, and I completed the project
because I partnered with two individuals (Mrs. Marion and
Ms. Chelsea) who, though never officially titled coaches,
gracefully played the role. I am profoundly grateful to
them today.

When I began collaborating with Mrs. Marion Weldon,
she immediately steered me in the right direction by
exchanging ideas after reading just one chapter of the
book. Her informal coaching inspired me to add two
essential sections to complete the book's content: Ikigai
and Logotherapy. Another pivotal coaching relationship
was with Chelsea St. Cyr, who, despite her official roles as
the graphic designer and editor, also played the coach role.
Her contributions were instrumental, underscoring the
importance of a personal coach to stay on track with our
goals.

My book project serves as a testament to the importance of
personal coaching in both professional development and
personal life enhancement. Having witnessed the success

of my plan execution due to my partnership with the two unofficial coaches during the book writing and publishing process, I have become a strong proponent of life and professional coaching. I strongly encourage you to acquire a coach for your personal goals, especially when you feel your life project is not moving in the right direction.

5. *Networking*

You should plan on networking with people in your field or those upon whom your success depends. When I started working at Humana, the then-sales director of the Miami-Dade office, whom I greatly respected and admired, took me out to lunch during my first week. He advised me to build twenty-five sources of referrals to succeed as a sales agent. This advice became the magic formula for my success. Networking is a powerful tool in advancing your career and climbing the professional ladder.

An effective way to network is to join a professional organization, which can significantly enhance your growth in your field. This allows you to connect with peers and provides opportunities to gain experience from one another. The membership fees for these organizations are generally well justified, given the benefits they offer. Additionally, social media platforms provide extensive networking opportunities in today's digital age. You can tailor your network to meet your specific needs and preferences by engaging on sites like LinkedIn, Instagram, and Facebook. Remember, the scope of your network often determines the extent of your success.

6. *General Skills Development*

Today, there are abundant opportunities to acquire new skills, either for free or at a minimal cost. Enhancing your skill set should be a primary goal as you identify areas for improvement in your career. Once these areas are identified, developing a plan to acquire the transferrable skills to remain competitive in the marketplace and accomplish your life's mission is crucial. Consider acquiring some of the following skills tailored to your personal life's mission and development needs:

- Leadership
- Management
- Conflict Resolution
- Team Building
- Multicultural Communication
- Coaching
- Training
- Mentoring
- Time Management
- Critical Thinking
- Problem Solving
- Digital Literacy
- Adaptability
- Communication Skills
- Emotional Intelligence
- Project Management
- Analytical Skills
- Customer Service
- Innovation and Creativity

- Financial Literacy
- Negotiation

Sometimes, as a professional or business owner, you might perceive training sessions as too costly. However, viewing these opportunities as investments that can lead to better pay, personal fulfillment, and enhanced competitiveness is significant. Whether you are pursuing a career or running your own business, investing in professional growth brings benefits such as income growth, increased competitiveness, and more opportunities in the marketplace.

7. *Health Maintenance Plan*

Frequently, individuals find their aspirations hampered by unforeseen health challenges. I passionately believe that cultivating a health maintenance plan is critical to safeguarding our personal missions. My dad's example underscores this principle—he promptly took action upon being advised to undergo pacemaker installation, prioritizing his mission despite health concerns. Indeed, health setbacks can profoundly impact our activities. To minimize such disruptions, consider implementing these strategies:

- Cultivate a balanced and nourishing diet.
- Engage in regular exercise, aiming for daily activity or at least five days a week.
- Establish a consistent walking routine to promote physical well-being.
- Educate yourself about various chronic conditions and adopt practices to mitigate associated risks.

- Assume full responsibility for monitoring and managing your health status.
- Select a trusted primary care physician with whom you can openly discuss your health concerns.
- Set aside time to decompress daily. You need relaxed moments during the day, away from regular work activities. I learned this from a friend in the military. When my wife and I visited her, she was doing the dishes late at night. My wife and I knew she was tired and suggested she go to bed, but she insisted she needed time to decompress. I realized I do the same with dishes to relieve stress. Decompressing with an activity that helps you burn calories is quite helpful.
- Schedule vacation time annually to recharge. While visiting exciting places is enjoyable, a vacation that takes you away from your regular work environment will suffice.

These proactive measures fortify physical well-being and strengthen our capacity to pursue and achieve our aspirations with resilience and vitality.

8. *Digital Literacy Development*

Being proficient in industry-specific software gives you a competitive edge in the marketplace and is invaluable whether you are an employee or an entrepreneur. Numerous digital tools are available for skills development and enhancing digital literacy, including platforms like

LinkedIn Learning and Udemy. My experience with several Udemy courses has significantly enriched the content presented in this book.

Setting specific goals for your digital literacy growth in relation to your career development is crucial. Write detailed objectives to improve your skills in key software such as Office 365, focusing primarily on Word, Excel, and Outlook; explore Adobe products; master a web browser of your choice, such as Chrome or Internet Explorer; and become acquainted with any other software essential to your field or industry.

Digital literacy has played a significant role in my success as a sales professional, manager, and writer. I advise you to learn how to use artificial intelligence to be more productive and competitive in your professional life or as an entrepreneur. Some people may argue that AI has some disadvantages, but it is a boat that I would not like you to miss.

To recap, your personal development plan should include specific goals on Professional Growth and Continuous Learning, People Skills Development, Mentor Acquisition, Coach Acquisition, Networking, General Skills Development, Health Maintenance, and Digital Literacy. A well-rounded skill set is crucial for enhancing your competitiveness in the marketplace, which can lead to greater earnings and further your personal mission.

The concluding section of Step 4 will allow you to build a mission-focused personal plan. This is vital to our focus because it represents a key goal of the MVP-PA model, creating the final set of directions needed to take mission-guided actions. I believe in your ability to transform your vision into a tangible reality.

The Mission-focused Personal Plan

Besides guiding forceful actions, a mission-focused personal plan is crucial to this journey of achievement. All the work we have been doing has been aimed at completing this plan. It should serve as your guide in life. You need a compass on the road to success, and the mission-focused personal plan fulfills that role beautifully by preparing you to take purposeful steps. Figure 10 captures the essence of the plan by showing all its main sections.

1. Mission Statement

We have thoroughly explored the concept of a personal mission. The personal mission statement defines the specific field you want to focus on and is crafted to be concise, leaving no room for distraction. This statement serves as the foundation of your mission-focused personal plan and underpins all other parts.

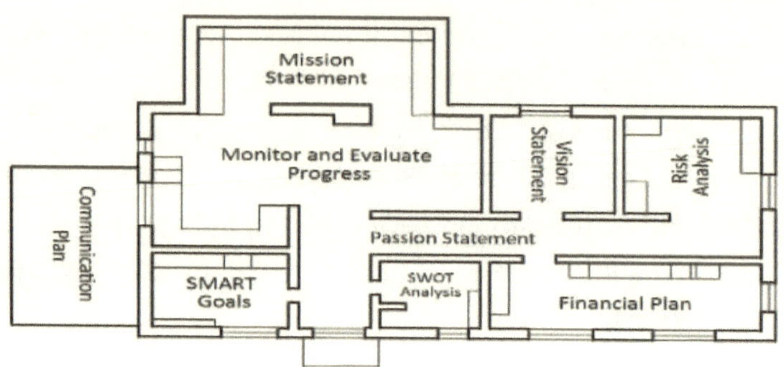

10Mission-Focused Personal Plan: A Roadmap to Achieve Your Mission

2. *Vision Statement*

The vision statement is a crucial part of your personal plan. You should have crafted one after reading Chapter 5, as it relates directly to your mission. Your personal vision statement should outline your aspirations and serve as the compass for your long-term goals.

3. *Passion Statement (Justification of the Plan; State Your Why)*

Creating a Passion Statement is critical in building your mission-focused personal plan.

4. SWOT Analysis

As previously discussed, dedicating time to thoroughly examining your strengths, weaknesses, opportunities, and threats is crucial. Document your findings comprehensively in this section. This detailed analysis will help you leverage your strengths, address your weaknesses, capitalize on your opportunities, and mitigate identified threats, enhancing your ability to successfully realize your mission-focused personal plan.

5. SMART Goals

You already know how to set SMART goals. In your mission-focused personal plan, it is essential to establish both long-term and short-term objectives. Short-term objectives serve as the foundation for achieving long-term goals. This process can be likened to constructing a house. Suppose we consider the house to be a long-term goal. In that case, we can break it down into short-term objectives with specific deadlines, such as hiring a general contractor, clearing the land, obtaining permits from the city, acquiring materials, laying the foundation, constructing the framework, installing electrical wiring, plumbing connections, and erecting walls, among others. I simplify this process because understanding goal setting and the importance of commitment distinguishes winners from losers. In some cases, in the business world, long-term goals are referred to as strategies, and short-term objectives as tactics, but the underlying principle remains unchanged. For each strategy, you must define a set of tactics. This systematic approach enables you to deconstruct a large goal into manageable smaller objectives. In the following section, consider these examples of long-term goals matched with short-term objectives:

Long-Term Goal:

- Increase access to trade schools for high school dropouts in County ABC, Florida, by 25% within the next five years.

Short-Term Objectives:

- Conduct a needs assessment in County ABC within the next three months to determine the current situation of targeted residents and the obstacles they face in accessing trade schools.
- Recruit professionals from the business world within the next six months to mentor and sponsor the targeted individuals.
- Maintain weekly sessions on career planning and access to trade schools within the next year.
- Secure funding from grants and donations within the next year to finance students interested in completing their training within the next five years.
- Work with trade schools within the next six months to customize three- to six-month training programs that provide access to employment.

Long-Term Goal:

- Based on key health indicators such as hypertension, diabetes management, and obesity rates, improve the health outcomes of people in underserved communities in County XYZ by 20% within the next five years.

Short-Term Objectives:

- Conduct a needs assessment of the population within the next three months to determine the barriers to accessing healthcare.
- Obtain data from health clinics and public hospitals in the county within the next three months on the percentage of people affected by hypertension, diabetes, and obesity.
- Secure funding for education workshops and radio programs within the next six months to educate the population on improving key health indicators.
- Design a project within the next three months for community clinics and public hospitals to collect data on their patients to track progress over the next five years.
- Open a healthy food distribution center in underserved communities within the next three months.

The next three sections cover communication, finance, and action plans. These plans align with components commonly found in business plans, such as marketing, financial, and operational plans.

6. *The Communication Plan (Strategies)*

The communication plan outlines strategies for presenting and marketing oneself to achieve personal and professional goals and reach the public and relevant stakeholders. The following strategies are suggested:

Personal Resume:

- Develop a well-crafted resume highlighting your mission, values, and relevant experiences.
- Tailor the resume to emphasize your connection with the mission and highlight accomplishments aligned with your goals.
- Nowadays, some people get creative with visual professional resumes and self-presentations.

One-to-One Communication with Key Stakeholders:

- Engage in personalized, one-on-one communication with key stakeholders, such as beneficiaries, sponsors, contributors, and support people to build relationships, gather feedback, and address specific needs and concerns.

Mass Media Communication and Social Media Platforms:

- Develop a strategic approach for mass media and social media engagement to amplify the message and reach a broader audience.
- Utilize platforms for media interviews and guest blogging opportunities.

Community Engagement and Outreach:

- Engage with local communities, grassroots organizations, and advocacy groups relevant to the mission.
- Participate in community events, volunteer activities, or outreach programs to raise awareness and contribute to positive change.
- Develop and facilitate educational workshops, training programs, or online courses relevant to the mission.

Feedback Mechanisms:

- Establish feedback mechanisms and channels for collecting input, suggestions, and criticism.
- Regularly solicit feedback through tools such as surveys, polls, focus groups, or direct communication to gauge effectiveness and identify areas for improvement.

These strategies encompass various approaches to communication and outreach, aiming to convey the mission effectively, engage stakeholders, and increase awareness.

7. *Financial Plan for Your Personal Mission*

The financial plan outlines strategies to secure funding for your personal mission.

Financial Asset Assessment:

- Conduct a thorough assessment of available financial assets, including personal funds allocated for the mission, to determine the current financial state and resources.

Personal Investment:

- Assess the feasibility of investing personal funds or relying on professional income to support the mission.

External Partnerships:

- Determine the support needed from external partners, including friends, family, organizations, and foundations, to finance the mission.

Grant Acquisition:

- Research and pursue grant opportunities as a potential funding source for the mission.

Loan Consideration:

- Explore the option of obtaining loans to finance the mission, considering the associated terms and risks.

Business Development:

- Evaluate the possibility of establishing a business entity to generate revenue dedicated to funding the personal mission.

Crowdfunding Initiatives:

- Utilize online platforms such as GoFundMe, Facebook, etc., to initiate crowdfunding campaigns and raise funds from a wider audience.

Donation Channels:

- Establish multiple donation channels, including secure website payments, PayPal, GoFundMe, Zelle payments, checks, and pledges, to facilitate contributions from supporters. For instance, a charity organization on whose board I serve runs an annual fundraising campaign. They utilize the following channels to collect donations: GoFundMe, the organization's website, PayPal, Zelle, Cash App, and personal checks.

Funding Strategies:

- Develop targeted strategies for securing funding from various sources, including friends, family, organizations, and potential donors, based on their interests and capacity to contribute. In the case of my dad's mission, he utilized friends and family members to fund educational scholarships for underprivileged students.

It is important to note that there are three primary ways to fund your personal mission:

- **Personal Wealth:** You can choose to be successful as a professional and use your personal wealth, especially your discretionary income, to fund your cherished mission.
- **Business Profits:** You can open a business and allocate some of its profits to finance your mission. A successful business can support its owner's mission through its earnings.
- **Nonprofit Organization:** You can create a nonprofit organization, commonly referred to as a 501(c)(3), to fund your mission.

These models are widely utilized today. For instance, Michael Bloomberg's donation of $1.8 billion to Johns Hopkins University for student financial aid is a notable example of using personal wealth to advance a personal mission in education. Many business owners, such as Bill Gates with the Bill & Melinda Gates Foundation, use business profits to support philanthropic efforts. Some friends of mine recently created a foundation that they will fund with their business profits to support educational projects. Additionally, countless nonprofit organizations have been established to further personal missions in various fields. The fiscal systems in the United States and many other countries allow these organizations to fund their missions through tax-deductible strategies.

As mentioned in Chapter 4, your profession does not have to be your mission, but it can be used to help you realize your mission.

8. Action Plan (Strategies)

Identifying Key Contributors:

- Identifying key contributors could translate into specific actions such as conducting stakeholder mapping, reaching out to potential partners, and establishing collaboration agreements.
- In many fields and companies, success often relies on your connections. Your advancement may depend on those who recognize and appreciate your personality, character, and skills. While not everyone will be a mentor, some connections can advocate for you during crucial decisions like promotions within your organization. Cultivate the habit of identifying people who can vouch for you. This principle remains relevant even if you are running your own business. There will be times when your success depends on your connections. Identifying individuals with influence, extensive knowledge, and industry connections can pave the way for your growth.

Determining the Need for a Business or Not-for-Profit Organization:

- This step involves conducting feasibility studies, legal research, and organizational planning to establish the appropriate structure to help you realize your mission. Please note that sometimes, you may even decide to work as an employee if your profession can produce enough capital to support your mission. The scope of your vision will determine the right course of action.

Setting Timelines:

- You should create a detailed project timeline with milestones and deadlines for each action step and initiative. I have experienced the value of timelines with this book project. My coach and professor, Marion Weldon, gracefully accepted the role of reading my writings one chapter at a time and helped me complete the publication project. Initially, I did not set any timeline for the publication besides the primary goal date of December 12, 2023, but I had already missed that original completion date. One day, I sent a piece of writing to her for suggestions, and in her response, she asked when I was planning to publish. To answer her question, I took the time to set timelines for each phase and sent them to her. Because I valued her time and knowledge, I decided to commit to these timelines. I asked my editor and designer to help me respect my deadlines. The project timelines allowed me to complete the manuscript in June 2024 simply because I set timelines for the publication. It is important to set timelines, but it is even more important to be committed to honoring the timelines you set for your plan. This book is a vivid example of this principle.

Determining Personnel Needs:

- This step involves defining roles and responsibilities, recruiting team members or volunteers, and providing training and support as needed.

Professional Licenses, Training, and Work Schedules:

- This section could be addressed by identifying required qualifications, arranging training programs, and establishing work schedules that align with mission priorities.

Please note that every mission is different. The action or operational plans will vary based on circumstances, environments, and needs. The action plan's function is to help you inventory the needed resources, such as human resources, materials, equipment, professional licenses, training, etc. It is important to ensure that your strategies consist of concrete action steps or initiatives that contribute to achieving your mission objectives effectively and efficiently.

9. *Risk Analysis*

Identify every potential obstacle to the success of your mission-focused personal plan. Consider the following risks:

- *Financial Risks:* Insufficient funding and unexpected expenses.
- *Time Management Risks:* Overcommitment, poor allocation.
- *Health Risks:* Burnout, illness.
- *Professional and Personal Development Risks:* Skill obsolescence, lack of network growth.
- *External Risks:* Economic changes, technological disruptions.
- *Strategic Risks:* Misalignment with mission, lack of flexibility.
- *Social and Cultural Risks*: Public perception, cultural shifts.

10. Monitor and Evaluate Progress

Use tools like spreadsheet software, e.g., Excel, to monitor and evaluate the functionality and progress of your mission-focused personal plan. Set a schedule to check progress monthly, quarterly, semi-annually, or annually. This is accomplished through regular control and reports, creating opportunities to adjust when necessary.

11. Corrective Actions

Progress reports facilitate the implementation of corrective actions. It is essential to schedule specific times for implementing these strategies. When conducted effectively, company meetings enable leaders and managers to set the tone for improving the trajectory of company plans and projects. You can apply this principle to your mission as well.

Drawing from my experience attending monthly sales meetings as a career sales agent at Humana Inc., I found these gatherings invaluable. Managers would outline improvement strategies and recognize sales agents for outstanding performance. This section emphasizes the importance of remaining flexible and adaptable, allowing you to make necessary adjustments based on insights gained or changing circumstances. However, if corrective actions are not implemented in response to the discrepancies identified in the reports, these reports will be deemed ineffective and unnecessary.

Below you will find an exercise challenging you to write your mission-focused personal plan. You are on the brink of achieving meaningful success. However, a plan holds no value without action. The time has come for you to prepare for action.

In our concluding chapter, we will explore the importance of taking action to pursue success with meaning. Pay special attention to this chapter, as your ability to take decisive action will greatly determine your success in accomplishing short and long-term goals while overcoming challenges.

Step 4 Exercise

1. Write a smart long-term goal for your chosen personal mission.
2. Write the short-term objectives that support the long-term goal.
3. Write a concise mission-focused personal plan:
4. Write:
   - a mission statement
   - a vision statement
   - a passion (justification or why) statement
5. Identify key contributors and stakeholders for your plan (beneficiaries, donors, sponsors, public officials, community leaders, networks, etc.)
6. Write:
   - a short communication plan
   - a short financial plan
   - a short action plan
7. Run a risk analysis.
8. State how you will monitor and evaluate progress.
9. State corrective actions.
10. Finalize the plan.

Chapter 8
Step 5: Take Action

"Vision without action is merely a dream. Action without vision just passes the time. Vision with action can change the world."[37]

– Joel A. Barker

A plan is only as good as the actions taken to execute it. Until you take decisive steps to bring your plan to fruition, the world remains unaware of your dream or vision. No matter how magnificent your vision, it cannot be defined by words alone. Your actions give substance to it; they are the tangible embodiment of your aspirations. If your dream is the spirit, your actions are the materialization of its body or at least a vital component thereof. Your actions bring you closer to your dream, allowing you to feel, sense, and touch the essence of your aspirations.

---

[37] Barker, Joel A. "Joel A. Barker Quotes." BrainyQuote. Accessed October 29, 2023. https://www.brainyquote.com/quotes/joel_a_barker_158200.

11Action: Steps that Solve Problems and Transform Dreams into Reality

While every component of the MVP-PA success model is essential, it is in the action stage that dreams are truly transformed into reality. Action breathes life into your mission, vision, passion, and plan. Through action, your vision materializes, becoming something tangible that people can witness and discuss. Although your plan consists of multiple actions and milestones, each step brings you closer to realizing your vision and manifesting your success. You can never truly know your ability to achieve something until you engage in purposeful action. Since multiple actions are needed to bring your vision to fruition, these are like the last bits of salt needed to prepare the food. Therefore, your daily actions must align with the mission guiding your plan.

You must approach your plan with persistence, confidence, and determination to execute it successfully. While some simple projects or experiences may allow for spontaneous action without a formal plan, most endeavors require a written plan that outlines the various milestones. The plan should guide your actions, although flexibility is crucial, as the execution may need to adapt to changing circumstances in the field. The recent experience of our generation with the COVID-19 crisis underscores the importance of flexibility in plan execution. Many reputable American universities had to adapt their operations due to the new environment, highlighting the need for contingency plans for unexpected events during plan execution.

How I Got My First Scholarship: The Power of Action

In October 1989, the beginning of my college journey in Port-au-Prince, Haiti, was a time of immense pressure. After graduating high school as both Valedictorian and School President, I often felt these titles were "two curses" that burdened me with high expectations. The fear of failure was not just a personal concern but a worry that my classmates might use it as an excuse not to strive for excellence. My family, too, had their hopes set high. Given these expectations, coupled with my high school's reputation as one of the best in the country, I was determined to work harder than the average student. I knew that having the dedication and putting in more work were necessary to secure my success as a professional. This journey, filled with challenges and triumphs, is a testament to the power of action and the potential it holds for us. It's a reminder that no matter the circumstances, with dedication and hard work, success is within reach.

During the very first hour of our college class, Mr. Frantz Theodat, my business math teacher, offered us some advice that he suggested we implement in our senior year. He advised us to identify a mentor in our field who could guide us toward professional success. Following his advice, at the start of my senior year, I sought the guidance of my cousin's boss, Jean-Paul, who was managing his family's business at the time. Though Jean-Paul was only a year older than me, he was twenty years older in terms of professional experience. He was already a successful professional and generously agreed to mentor me.

In April 1993, I found a job posting requiring a master's degree for a director's position at a not-for-profit organization. Despite not having completed my undergraduate studies, my drive for success convinced me that I possessed the necessary skills for the job. I did not own a computer and had minimal experience with one. I had only visited the business school computer lab once and the computer I used that day wasn't even operational. Nonetheless, I knew someone who could make it happen: my mentor, Jean-Paul. I quickly gathered all the necessary information to craft my resume. I included every piece of experience I had acquired since high school, along with all the seminars I attended and my accomplishments, ensuring the recruiter would understand the breadth of skills I offered. A director's role demands robust skills; I was determined to demonstrate mine. After completing my resume, I headed to the factory where my mentor worked. He was not there initially, but I waited patiently and hopefully. Upon his arrival, I explained my situation and eagerness for the job. I initially asked him if his administrative assistant could type up my resume. He chose to type it himself in a surprising and fortunate turn of events—an honor and a joy. He sat down at his computer and began to work on my resume. Watching him generously offer his assistance, I felt God was speaking through him. In his generous tone, he said, "You have an interesting resume; I will help you get a scholarship."

As promised, my mentor contacted a group that managed a full two-year scholarship program for Central American and Caribbean students to study in American community colleges as exchange students. This program aimed to equip students with knowledge and skills they could share in their home countries upon their return. The group invited me to apply, and I submitted my application. They approved my application for the scholarship. My joy was boundless, like a child receiving his favorite ice cream. Reflecting on the opportunity the scholarship created for me, I conclude today that the lesson I should learn is: if you cannot get the job you desire, you must improve your skill set to increase your employment prospects. In addition, you should always believe that you deserve excellent opportunities.

Before our group traveled to America, we spent three days at a pleasant hotel for an orientation to prepare us for our new experiences and to learn about American culture. The office responsible for selecting the applicants in Haiti hired a psychology professor, Dr. Roseline Benjamin, to enhance our interpersonal communication skills. During these sessions, we delved into various aspects of American culture and the essential elements needed to integrate into the American school system successfully.

Every student took away lessons that would last a lifetime from these sessions. I personally retained two key insights. First, I learned that Americans generally prefer maintaining personal space during conversations—a contrast to Haitian and some other cultures, where proximity is the norm during interactions. This understanding was crucial as culturally in Haiti, being physically close during a conversation is often seen as necessary for clear communication.

Second, the trainer introduced us to transactional analysis, which outlines three types of personas—parent, child, and adult—that can emerge during interpersonal communications. The theory emphasizes that the healthiest communication occurs when we express ourselves as adults. This means communicating facts without excessive emotion or casting blame, akin to a parent reprimanding a child. By staying objective, we avoid making judgments or seeking favors, facilitating clearer and more effective interactions.

The three-day orientation at the hotel marked an early transition from a life of financial constraints to an experience of abundance. Growing up, I had limited access to technology. I remember using a telephone for the first time when I was around sixteen years old. Education was my dad's priority, and it wasn't until late in high school that we had a TV set at home. Despite these limitations, I found joy in other aspects of life. I loved camping and the adventures of climbing mountains with family and friends. I often spent four hours walking to my grandparents' home in the mountains of Leogane, my hometown in Haiti, during the summertime. I cherished playing with other kids in the rivers, spending fun days at the beach, playing soccer, dominoes, and cards, among other games. And surprisingly, I loved going to church and praying. My happiness was deeply rooted in my interactions with people and the natural world around me.

The big day finally arrived: August 13th, 1993. I traveled from Port-au-Prince, Haiti, to the city of Seattle, marking my first time leaving Haiti and my first time flying. My initial stop was Miami International Airport, where I was awash with emotions—happiness, surprise, perplexity, yet confident about a promising future. The contrast was stark; in Haiti, I had to walk from the airport facility to the airplane, whereas Miami Airport boasted the convenient jet bridges we are all accustomed to today. In Miami, I met other students from Central America and the Caribbean. Together, we traveled to Dallas before catching our final flight to Seattle. This journey was unique. Upon arrival,

Diane, my host mother in America, warmly welcomed me and provided an unforgettable greeting. On my first day, I inadvertently locked the bathroom door after using it—a silly mistake but a memorable part of settling in. In Diane's house, I lived with Sylvan, a French student who translated my poetic introduction letter to Diane and helped me navigate the unfamiliar environment, and Risa, a kind student from Japan, whose presence meant I was spared from cooking duties. I also had three host sisters who made me feel incredibly welcome. I enrolled in the business program at Edmonds Community College in Lynnwood, Washington, just a short distance from Seattle. This opportunity gave me excellent English, management, technology, and multicultural communication skills. I made friends from around the globe, including Thailand, Japan, Brazil, France, Indonesia, Germany, etc. Moreover, I had the chance to display my paintings at the school's annual art exhibit, and I was also selected to be photographed for the school's advertising materials. This honor underscored my involvement and presence at the institution.

After completing the program, I returned to Haiti in August 1995. I secured my first job after one month in the Ministry of Culture through my connections as an advisor to the Minister (Secretary) of Culture. However, the secretary had to let me go as I was unprepared for the administrative chaos and the political nature of the job.

In January 1996, I found a job advertisement like the one I saw in April 1993. I applied for a Purchasing Director's position and was hired, realizing that my strong resume and the recruiter's familiarity with my mentor significantly influenced this decision.

I joined the management team at International Child Care, an organization that has been operating in Haiti since 1967. Their mission is to raise funds in both the U.S. and Canada to support community health projects in Haiti, with a primary focus on tuberculosis. This role effectively replaced the director's position I had initially applied for in 1993.

As you can see, the scholarship that brought me to study in America proved to be a pivotal life opportunity, granting me an advantageous position in Haiti. My decisive actions were crucial in launching my career on an exceptional path.

From a $4 Investment to an Accomplished Artist

One seemingly mundane decision at a small bookstore in Port-au-Prince, Haiti, in 1989—purchasing a book titled *"L'Art et le Vivant: Eveil a la Creation,"* translated into English as "Art and Life: Awakening to Creation" for just $4—marked the beginning of an extraordinary journey into the world of art. This book introduced me to the concept of spirals as movements of the body and art as a means of personal and spiritual growth. Inspired, I drew spirals, starting from a single point and expanding in a continuous spiral motion, eventually returning to the initial point. These sketches, filled in with black pencils, laid the foundation of my artistic exploration.

Recognizing the potential in these early works, my brother Hendrick encouraged me to pursue formal training, which led me to enroll in the National School of Arts in Haiti. However, political unrest at the school prematurely ended my formal art education, turning what seemed like a setback into a blessing in disguise. This disruption forced me to continue my artistic exploration independently, allowing me to delve deeper into my soul and heart to discover my true self. I began using gouache during this period, creating pieces that resonated well with my peers and were praised for their originality and uniqueness.

The pinnacle of my journey occurred in 1994 when my painting, Evolution, was selected for the cover page of *Between the Lines*, a book displaying artworks from students at Edmonds Community College in Lynnwood, Washington. This achievement, akin to winning the first prize at an art contest, validated my artistic endeavors and affirmed my status as a gifted artist.

Although I have not yet commercialized my art, considering it a hobby until I can sell a piece for a million dollars, this moment solidified my belief in the importance of action and passion. Success in art, as in life, is not solely measured by commercial transactions but by the impact and recognition one's work achieves. My journey underscores that taking even the smallest step towards pursuing your passion can lead to profound achievements, transforming simple actions into magical outcomes.

Now Carries the Power of Transformation

It was a transformative moment for me when, during a birthday party, I witnessed a true embodiment of success with meaning. André, the uncle of more than twelve young professionals, was honored with a recognition plaque for his significant contributions to the success of his nephews and nieces. André was one of my mentors when I was growing up in Haiti, and he currently owns and manages a multi-service firm in South Florida. I have always admired his sense of mission, leadership, and action for his relatives and community.

Additionally, a successful young professional named Joseph presented him with another plaque on behalf of Notre Dame of Lourdes Elementary School Alumni. My dad's scholarship project, which I mentioned earlier in this book, supports the same school. Joseph mentioned that André remains the most impactful person in his life because his achievements are mainly due to André's leadership and the creation of the school in their village. Many of these young professionals, who became successful in their professions, acknowledged that they might have been working on farms, generating modest incomes, without André's efforts to start the school project.

I cried tears of joy and emotions that day, realizing how impactful André's life has been in transforming the lives of so many people. His mission to improve the lives of his family members and those in my dad's home village has made a significant difference. André's actions were crucial when he created the school because his favorable circumstances regarding the opportunity changed at some point. The school project could have been aborted if he had not acted when he had the idea.

I had a long and enriching conversation with André, during which he taught me a valuable lesson about action. According to him, you should take immediate action when you have an idea about a project. The power of transformation lies in the present moment, and your project idea cannot be executed by someone else. You are the only one who can successfully bring that idea to life. I would add that the idea that comes to you is like an inspiration from Universal Intelligence, and your job is to act now to bring it to fruition until you reach the top of the achievement pyramid, where you can celebrate your project's realization.

Now is always the perfect moment to take action. While the model contains five powerful steps, actions are humans' main and most effective tools for transforming lives and developing communities and countries. Your passion for your mission, vision, and plan is greatly important, but *success with meaning* becomes tangible only through transformational actions.

Get Out of Your Comfort Zone: Embrace Challenges

The paradox of comfort and adversity in personal growth is profound and complex. While comfort may seem appealing, it often leads to stagnation. Remember, pressure makes diamonds; without applying pressure to push beyond your limits, your success will remain confined. Engaging in the battle against your comfort is the first step toward carving your path to success. It is crucial to step out of that attractive comfort zone and confront the fires of adversity. Despite having everything you might need, there is always room to explore new heights and intensify your quest for a richer life experience, marked by significant achievements and impactful contributions to a better world.

Observations reveal that those individuals from affluent backgrounds, despite their abundant resources—nutritious food, endless entertainment, and extensive support from eager parents—often fail to reach the expected peaks of success. This comfort paradoxically dampens their drive to excel. In contrast, those from less privileged backgrounds display remarkable resilience and determination, often outperforming their more privileged counterparts. This exhibited disparity highlights how adversity fuels growth and ambition, catalyzing profound personal development.

The proverbs "Pressure makes diamonds" and "A bird in a cage will forget how to fly" powerfully illustrate the necessity of embracing challenges. Adversity hones our abilities and nurtures resilience, reminding us that true growth requires overcoming hardships. Comfort, while seductive, leads to complacency, eroding our skills and dampening our survival instincts.

Growing up, I observed two individuals who faced a pivotal decision: leave the familiar comforts of the countryside for educational opportunities in Port-au-Prince. The first individual found it challenging to adapt to city life, particularly the irregular availability of food. Overwhelmed by the discomfort, he chose to return to the countryside, forfeiting the opportunity to pursue higher education and a potentially lucrative career. The second individual, however, embraced the discomfort of leaving his comfort zone. Despite the challenges of adapting to a new environment, he completed high school, progressed to university, and eventually established a successful construction company in Port-au-Prince, Haiti. His journey illustrates the transformative power of stepping out of one's comfort zone, leading to personal growth and professional success far beyond what the countryside could offer.

Embracing pressure and stepping out of comfort zones are beneficial and essential. Remaining within comfort zones is comparable to a complacent team that has achieved success but stops practicing, only to be overtaken by more driven competitors. Challenges are not merely obstacles; they are opportunities for greatness. Without the drive to improve continuously, becoming a champion remains a distant dream.

Consider the example of a sales team: the sales agents under pressure to meet personal obligations often outperform their more secure colleagues. This drive, born from necessity, leads to exceptional results. Similarly, letting fear paralyze you only stifles your potential for exploration and growth. To achieve your mission, you must conquer fear, embrace failure as a stepping stone, and act decisively.

The comfort zone is a fierce enemy of progress. Holding to comfort limits your ability to innovate and execute new projects. Progress favors the bold—the ones willing to face challenges and take risks, knowing their efforts will yield rewards.

Now is the time to act with the confidence that fosters success. Step out of your comfort zone and ascend to new heights of achievement and fulfillment. By daring to venture beyond the familiar confines of safety, you unlock your true potential, enabling you to forge a legacy that resonates profoundly and endures across humanity. Embrace your mission, pursue your vision, and achieve your goals—act now. The time is ripe, and the opportunities are boundless. Keep in mind that these opportunities are reserved for those brave enough to step beyond the bounds of their comfort zones and seize the infinite power of the present moment.

Decision-Making Models

The fear of making mistakes can often lead to analysis paralysis, where we endlessly analyze without taking decisive action. This fear, if not overcome, can stagnate our lives. The most significant risk in any situation is failing to act. Instead of allowing fear to immobilize us, we should cultivate a habit of proactive problem-solving. A reliable decision-making model is crucial for confidently addressing challenges, especially when we are uncertain about how to proceed. Trusting our intuition can yield positive results when confronted with a crisis or problem, but it is not always guaranteed. Because of this, I want to share with you a straightforward decision-making process I learned many years ago.

When confronted with a problem, consider the following steps:

1. Brainstorm potential solutions.
2. Select a few options that you believe are the best.
3. Create two columns for each selected option.
4. In the first column, list the advantages; in the second, list the disadvantages.
5. Review all options and choose the one with the most advantages and the fewest disadvantages.

Having a decision-making model is invaluable. The model I currently use is value-driven, which I learned in my business administration classes at Nova Southeastern University. In a value-driven decision-making process, we consider all stakeholders affected by the decision and lay out different options. The option to choose is the one that brings the most value and the least burden to each group of stakeholders in an optimal way. There are many other decision-making models available. The key is to adopt a frame of reference to guide us in our decision-making process, preventing analysis paralysis that can hinder our progress in life and negatively impact personal or organizational effectiveness.

Action vs. Procrastination

Some individuals find themselves delaying the pursuit of their dreams or failing to act altogether as if opportunities will always wait for them. Procrastination can indeed be a formidable adversary, diminishing the number of projects from which the world can benefit. The longer one procrastinates, the further success or project completion is delayed. Therefore, our mantra should be "Action and Action Now," as succumbing to the devil of procrastination can impede our success or hinder our ability to overcome challenges.

It is easy to assume we have an eternity to act upon our missions, but the reality can be sobering. The constraints of mortality bind our journey on this earth; even the longest lifespan stretches to a mere 120 years for the fortunate few. Yet, even with such longevity, maintaining the physical capability to continue nurturing our missions is no guarantee.

I believe in setting a timeline for realizing our missions, aiming to embark upon our purpose before age fifty and consolidating our position until age sixty-five. How often have we harbored an idea, only to watch as someone else seized upon it and brought it to fruition? Procrastination, we must realize, is a luxury we cannot afford. Opportunities, once lost, may never return, leaving us to regret our hesitance.

As custodians of our dreams, we must cultivate the habit of decisive action. We must summon the courage to act on our convictions and aspirations even amidst uncertainty. Progress is an expression of purposeful action; it requires the proactive steps of those who dare to confront the unknown with unwavering resolve and confidence, aiming to make a difference and impact the world.

In this very moment, we hold the power to bestow upon the world the gift entrusted to our lives. It falls upon us to ensure that we do not depart this world with our purpose unfulfilled, leaving behind only the echo of untapped potential.

Every conviction stirring within us, every impulse of goodness demanding expression, and every desire to make a difference require our immediate attention. We must dismantle the shackles of fear and perfectionism, for our actions can build the perfection we envision. We cannot simply be bystanders in life's performance but must become active participants, shaping our destinies with every action we undertake.

I implore you not to wait for the stars to align or for certainty to reveal. Seize the moment, embrace the now, and let your actions speak volumes. Through bold and unwavering action, we can fulfill our mission and leave a legacy for the world.
The power of realization lies in the **now**. The time to act and make a difference is **now**.

Adversity: A Steppingstone to Achievement

There will be moments when you feel like you are teetering on the edge, moments when giving up seems like the easiest option. But resist that urge. In these moments of adversity, the true depth of your potential can shine. Overcoming obstacles allows us to unearth our true strength and resilience.

Consider obstacles not as roadblocks but as disguised opportunities. They are gifts in disguise, catalysts for growth and development. As humanity evolves and becomes stronger when faced with challenges, so do you. Diamonds form only under high pressure and temperature. If you consciously understand the diamond formation process, you will welcome your life's downturns and weather the storms until you surface to greater achievement. Be aware of your potential for transformation. Every time you face an obstacle, it becomes an opportunity to shine.

Embrace the opportunity of adversity to display your inner fortitude. This is your chance to prove to yourself how strong and courageous you are. Stand tall, face your challenges head-on, and let them be the steppingstones that propel you toward extraordinary achievement.

Focus More on What You Can Control

After closing my mortgage company amidst the 2008 real estate crisis, I attended a job search seminar in Coral Springs, FL, where the gracious woman trainer shared invaluable insights. She wisely pointed out the futility of fretting over the economy, as it lies beyond our control. Instead, she encouraged us to focus on what we can influence: refining the presentation of our resumes, honing our interview skills, fostering professional development, and maintaining a positive attitude. Notably, we can shape our interactions with managers, colleagues, and subordinates. By prioritizing these controllable elements and consistently pursuing excellence in our tasks and duties, success is bound to follow.

Remember, taking action—even if it fails—is far preferable to inaction, which leads to a dead end. Every action yields a positive or negative result, and each contributes to a forward trajectory. Ultimately, every action, even those with unwanted results, brings us closer to a better situation than before.

Decisive Moments Shape Our Success

Every crash needs immediate action. In 1978, at nine, I was considered the most accomplished student of the 1975-1976 school year at my neighborhood elementary school. My parents had such faith in my abilities that they decided to have me skip two grades. However, over the following two years, I developed a reputation as a poor and underperforming student. 1978 marked a significant downturn in my elementary school journey. From being the top student, I plummeted to one of the worst, failing a class twice. Recognizing my potential, my dad took decisive action. Leveraging his connections, he arranged for me to transfer to the next grade level at a public school in our neighborhood, effectively putting me back on track.

I share this story to encourage you to take action to change any undesirable circumstances. Just as my dad believed in me, I believe in you, and I am confident you are equipped to accomplish extraordinary things.

In 1993, as a senior student at a public university in Haiti, aged twenty-four, I faced a pivotal moment where I needed to chart my path to success. Drawing from my dad's principle of action, I contacted my cousin's boss, Mr. Jean Paul, and requested him to become my mentor. This bold step resulted in a two-year full scholarship to study in America and immerse myself in American culture. This scholarship, obtained through proactive measures, became my ticket to success, marking the second time that the principle of action had yielded significant rewards.

Fast forward to 2008, thirty years after my childhood school crisis, the economic downturn significantly impacted my financial situation. The situation seemed dire with two mortgages due to the ownership of an investment property, approximately five credit cards, and various financial obligations. My company, Memphis Mortgage, my sole source of income, could not generate any revenue. To make matters worse, my wife lost her job. Despite these challenges, I remained resilient, reassuring my wife that we would weather the storm. Rather than allowing the crash to defeat me, I took decisive action and transformed the setback into a triumphant comeback.

My dad and I did not wait for ideal conditions. We took immediate action to transform adversity into achievement, which exemplifies the power of action in transforming adversities into accomplishments.

I implore you to take action now in your personal and professional endeavors. Do not allow fear to paralyze you or hinder your progress toward success. Do not wait for a perfect sky to turn today's crash into an opportunity.

By making a habit of taking daily actions aligned with your mission and goals, you will secure success as a lifelong enterprise. The time to make things happen is always now. This is what I refer to as the principle of action.

It Is Time for Action

"The sky is the limit," as the saying goes, but reaching it requires more than just ambition. It requires a clear mission, a passionate vision, a detailed plan, and a decisive set of actions. This approach echoes what John F. Kennedy envisioned for America when he ambitiously laid out his plan to reach the moon. It's not just about desiring to reach the sky; it's about having a clear direction and a burning desire to act to get there.

Life is measured not by the dreams you nurture but by your actions. A clear mission is crucial; it anchors your endeavors. A vision statement is a beacon, outlining your path and illuminating your journey. Passion fuels the drive to execute your plans, while a well-crafted plan provides a comprehensive roadmap equipped with all necessary resources, strategies, and tactics for effective execution. However, action is where realization truly begins. While the initial steps are essential, establishing a daily habit of taking action almost guarantees that you will leave a significant mark on this planet.

You are responsible for making today perfect, which requires your mission-focused action. There is no substitute for action in the quest for success. As in sports, you can score if you shoot the ball; your chances drop to zero if you hesitate. I am convinced that for some individuals, their current homelessness stems from a moment of inaction when faced with critical issues like job loss or financial instability. In these pivotal moments, immediate action can make all the difference. Whether seeking new employment opportunities or addressing mounting credit card debt, taking proactive steps can prevent a situation from spiraling out of control.

Swift and decisive action is critical to managing challenges and securing stability. In the game of life, the only sure way to fail is by not acting. Leaders may have clear missions and visions, but it's the actions they take that define them and leave a lasting legacy. Every action you take brings you closer to your vision, making it essential for you to pursue your impactful mission consistently. The time is now, and you must act.

Step 5 Exercises

1. *List Five Actions That You Will Take in the Next Three Months*

- Actions are to be based on your goals.
- Break down each goal into smaller, actionable tasks.
- Set deadlines for each task to keep yourself accountable.
- Schedule regular check-ins to review progress and adjust as needed.
- Prioritize tasks based on urgency and importance.

2. *Immediate Actions*

- Brainstorm ideas related to your mission or project.
- Research relevant information or resources online.
- Create a rough outline or plan for your next steps.
- Reach out to potential collaborators or mentors for advice or support.
- Set up a dedicated workspace or organize materials for your project.
- Hire a coach or explore coaching options through social media and online platforms.
- Polish your resume or your business plan.

3. *Small Daily Actions*

- Spend 15 minutes each day exploring innovative ideas or practical solutions.

- Review your progress in relation to your goals before starting your day.
- Take a 10 to 15-minute break to stretch and relax your mind.
- Read at least 5 minutes about your mission or field of interest.
- Practice positive affirmations to boost your motivation, attitude, and confidence in your quest for success and happiness.

Conclusion

Leveraging the MVP-PA Model for a Life of Success with Meaning

In the vast symphony of life, where everyone contributes a unique melody, the importance of having a personal mission cannot be overstated. This profound yet often overlooked truth is the cornerstone of a life lived not just existentially but with purpose and meaning. My dad's life beautifully exemplifies this principle. Although education was not his profession, it was truly his mission. His commitment to education transcended conventional measures of success, such as material wealth. Through his example, I learned that true success is not measured by financial prosperity but by our tangible, positive impact on the world. If success and wealth do not contribute positively to the lives of others, they become irrelevant. Thus, the real measure of success should be gauged by the impact one makes—an influence that inevitably leads to a fulfilling life of achievement. *Success with meaning* benefits humanity and drives personal accomplishment for mission-driven people who take action.

The journey toward understanding and embracing this kind of success begins with defining a personal mission. Every individual possesses a unique talent or passion that can contribute significantly to the harmony of humanity. Nevertheless, a mission can lack direction without clearly articulating its aspirations. It is here that aspirations transform from dreams into tangible goals. The MVP-PA model I introduced in this book remains invaluable in this transformation. This model helps structure these aspirations within a sharp vision, turning passion into a strategic action plan. Once this vision is articulated and the passion for achieving these goals is ignited, a pathway toward real success is set in motion.

Personal responsibility is an essential element in this equation. Our journey through this book has underscored the significance of being accountable, not only to oneself but also to the broader community. Personal responsibility is the bedrock of the MVP-PA model, manifesting as love in action—an imperative force that drives us to care for ourselves and others actively. This concept of responsibility extends beyond mere self-discipline and integrity; it encompasses a comprehensive suite of virtues, including ethical behavior, accountability, altruism, perseverance, thoughtfulness, continuous self-improvement, and diligence. These virtues are crucial as they enable individuals to contribute vigorously to planet Earth's and humanity's welfare.

To effectively illustrate how these concepts converge to define success, let us consider the structure of the ultimate achievement journey. It should ideally include:

1. *A Personal Development Plan*

    This plan should encompass elements such as self-awareness through a personal SWOT analysis, setting SMART goals, securing mentorship, developing partnerships with coaches, enhancing people skills, pursuing professional growth, and engaging in continuous learning. Networking, maintaining health, and developing digital literacy are also crucial components that prepare individuals for the challenges and opportunities ahead.

2. *A Mission-Focused Plan*

Incorporating the five pillars of the MVP-PA success model is vital. This includes:

- A mission statement that defines your field of intervention or purpose.
- A vision statement that articulates your aspirations.
- A passion statement that justifies your pursuit of this mission and vision.
- An integrated plan that includes SMART goals and defines communication, finance, and action strategies necessary for realizing the mission.
- A set of daily actions aimed at the realization of the mission.

The sky is the limit, but having a mission, a passionate vision, a plan, and a set of actions is what propels you there. John F. Kennedy set this example for America with his ambitious plan to reach the moon—a vision realized years after his time.

Where you start is not crucial; the unwavering focus on your destination matters. Achievement and greatness belong to those driven by a mission-focused vision and an unshakeable commitment. When commitment is steadfast, individuals establish a plan that demands action. These actions are pursued daily until the mission is accomplished.

Your mission must be clearly defined. You should know how you want your life to be remembered. Clarity in your mission and understanding it will help you effectively determine your vision. A clear mission is essential as it sets the tone for the entire process of achieving *success with meaning* through the application of the MVP-PA model. Essentially, your mission is what remains after you pass away. I actively live out this principle in my personal life.

For example, I recently discussed this with the priest overseeing the parish school that my dad supported through his scholarship program. I humorously mentioned that the school sponsorship is the legacy my dad left me, compelling me to continue funding the mission even after his death. This exemplifies a mission that endures beyond one's lifetime, making our lives eternally impactful.

Furthermore, total commitment to our mission is vital. This unwavering dedication is the only way to ensure our mission's realization. Commitment signifies our passion for our life mission and drives its achievement. The clarity in our vision engenders passion, which is crucial for committing to a well-designed plan and its execution. Ultimately, clarity is critical; it demonstrates the level of focus of the person living the mission and enhances the prospects of driving the mission to success.

The culmination of this book is not just the end of a reading experience but the beginning of a practical application of its teachings. Like Kennedy's moonshot, your visions and missions should be ambitious and transformative for yourself and the world.

Throughout my life, I have witnessed the power of focused, mission-driven success. My dad's intervention during my educational struggles and the dramatic shift in my career following the 2008 economic downturn are prime examples. Each pivotal moment was guided by clear, decisive action rooted in a profound sense of purpose. These experiences have taught me a vital lesson: true success stems from focused, purpose-driven actions.

As we draw this book to a close, I invite you to ponder the lessons shared and integrate them into your life actively. The path to a meaningful, impactful life is paved with your actions today, guided by your mission, driven by your passion, and structured by your plan.

Let this book be a catalyst for that journey. Whether you are seeking to redefine your professional path, enhance your personal life, or contribute to societal well-being, remember that success is a multifaceted achievement. It encompasses personal satisfaction, the positive impact you have on others, and the legacy you create.

Remember, the journey toward success does not stop at what you might consider a culminating point. Success is an ongoing process that demands continuous learning and refinement of your craft. Never rest on your laurels, thinking you have reached the pinnacle. There is no ultimate peak in the pursuit of excellence. Cultivate a daily habit of learning—it does not always come from books or classrooms. Engage in learning through conversations with peers, customers, children, and friends. Active listening during these interactions can unlock new and thought-provoking ideas. You may miss informal yet valuable lessons when you fail to listen actively. Observation is another powerful learning tool. Often, subtle details in events, activities, and interactions can offer profound insights and inspiration. Stay open to current ideas, even those that challenge your current perspectives, as they can lead to significant personal growth. Today, you have more opportunities; you can learn right from the comfort of your home using your computer, phone, or TV set. AI capability is making learning even more accessible because artificial intelligence can be an excellent teaching tool when you know how to use it.

Life is an inexhaustible wellspring of knowledge, available to you at every moment. Learn as naturally as you breathe, aiming to inspire others with your journey. Continuously hone your skills for as long as your mind allows. Live to learn, grow, succeed meaningfully, impact lives, and leave a legacy for humanity. Maintain your passion for learning and continual self-improvement. Just like a company cannot rest on its laurels, you must not assume that your skill set is complete and that you no longer need to improve.

One aspect I admire about the MVP-PA model is that it starts with MVP. In professional sports, whether in the NBA or the NFL, you cannot remain an MVP without constant self-improvement. Every MVP works daily to maintain their superiority and status. This is what I seek in you. I aim to awaken the giant within you so that the world can benefit from the champion inside you.

Reflect on your mission, clarify your vision, ignite your passion, plan strategically, and act boldly. The journey toward *success with meaning* is yours to undertake. It promises personal fulfillment and the opportunity to make a significant difference in people's lives.

Let's embark on this journey together, with the MVP-PA model as our guide, and transform our aspirations into achievements. Let's toast to achieving meaningful success, living purposefully, and making each day a step toward creating a better world. Together, we can and will achieve greatness. All we need is to take daily actions to transform our mission into a living reality.

You possess a powerful brain, regardless of personal or external perceptions, which makes you an incredible individual. With this potential, you have access to some of the greatest opportunities in the workplace. You have the capacity to establish one of the most successful businesses on the planet, lead the greatest not-for-profit organization, or become an outstanding professional. If you have reached this point in the book, with the right vision and passion, you hold the power to emulate figures like Thomas Edison, Bill Gates, Alexander Graham Bell, Mother Teresa, Richard Branson, Jeff Bezos, Elon Musk, Michael Bloomberg, and many others. I can assure you that none of these individuals are inherently smarter than you or me. What sets them apart is their integrated approach to the five proven steps to lifetime success: having a mission, vision, passion, plan, and taking bold actions. If you dare to dream big and follow the MVP-PA model, you CAN accomplish anything.

Commit to acting daily for your mission starting now. Remember, you can read all the books in the world and participate in all the seminars, workshops, and webinars, but you will never experience success or *success with meaning* if you do not get out of your comfort zone and take action. If you want *success with meaning*, you need to build your life on two major pillars: focus and action. Mission + vision + passion + plan equals focus. Being focused is your foundation in bringing your mission to life. This focus requires firm action to complete the recipe for achievement.

Be aware of the impact of your imagination and creativity in finding solutions for your life challenges. Take action to make your achievement pyramid a reality. Make your life worth living with a constant devotion to your transformative mission, and act resolutely to leave a legacy of greatness for the world. I truly aspire to shake friendly and proud hands with you at the top of the achievement pyramid.

To conclude our collective journey, I leave you with the achievement pyramid outlining our steps to achieve *success with meaning*. I encourage you to remain focused, act boldly, and embrace bravery for outstanding achievement and a lasting impact.

Achievement Pyramid

From Idea to Celebration of Achievement

It has been a pleasure to embark on this transformative reading journey with you. I am always fascinated by a commitment to success, action, and achievement. I nurture one dream for you: the dream of extraordinary performance in your life's journey. It is necessary to share with you the achievement pyramid, which illustrates how a single idea can be transformed into exceptional performance through focus (dream, mission, vision, passion, plan), action, and corrective measures.

You can construct your achievement pyramid through smart goal setting, effective planning, and mission-focused actions. The MVP-PA success model is yours to use for transformative achievement. Make the following pyramid part of your vision board; it will inspire you to work daily toward outstanding achievement. Enjoy the power and fulfillment of success with meaning.

Stages of the Achievement Pyramid

1. **Idea:** The first flash of inspiration
2. **Dream:** A broad aspiration of what you want to achieve.
3. **Mission:** A clear commitment or purpose derived from the dream, providing a unique and well-defined focus.
4. **Vision:** A detailed picture of what you aim to achieve within the scope of your mission.

5. **Passion:** The personal and inner motivation that creates enthusiasm, commitment, and persistence toward achieving the mission's outcomes.
6. **Goals/Objectives:** Specific milestones that originate from the vision.
7. **Plan/Project:** The chart of actionable steps to achieve the goals and objectives linked to the aspirational vision.
8. **Action:** The actual execution of the plan, transforming goals, concepts, objectives, strategies, and tactics into reality.
9. **Corrective Actions/Measures:** Adjustments made to maintain alignment with goals and the overall mission.
10. **Achievement:** The successful actualization of goals, fulfilling the mission.
11. **Celebration:** Acknowledging and rewarding the accomplishment with a noticeable sense of satisfaction, reinforcing meaning and purpose.

That's a wonderful illustration of the transformative journey of achievement, which I was inspired to call *success with meaning.*

Achievement Pyramid

12Achievement Pyramid: From Ideas to Achievements

Acknowledgments

First, I am grateful for the guidance and inspiration shaping my journey. This book would not have been possible without the support, wisdom, and strength drawn from a higher power. It also reflects the love and encouragement I have received from countless individuals throughout my life. I am deeply grateful to the world, and especially to the following people:

Family

- My beloved dad, the late Andre Robert Louis-Jacques, whose life story is my primary source of inspiration and to whom this book is dedicated.

- My loving and caring mother, the late Lina Bazile, who instilled in me the importance of treating everyone with love and respect.

- My great uncle, the late Mentor Bazile, whose unwavering positive attitude and exceptional people skills amazed me.

- My beloved grandmother, the late Flavie Francois, who took care of me in a unique way and made me feel like a prince.

- My beloved wife and soulmate, Shirley Thebaud Louis-Jacques, the cornerstone of my daily life, who insisted that I ensure the publication of a quality book.

- My brother, Hendrick Louis-Jacques, who is always loving, supportive, and proud. He encouraged my artistic pursuits by suggesting I attend art school.

- My siblings, whose love and appreciation have always inspired and strengthened me.

- My relatives, including uncles, aunts, cousins, nephews, and nieces, all of whom have made me feel truly special.

- My wife's family and relatives who never stopped showing me love and appreciation, including my wife's nieces Samantha and Nerissa, whom I consider my daughters.

- My children, Karl-Stephane and Veronique, my daily inspirations. I hope you carry forward the lessons from your grandfather, find your missions, and achieve *success with meaning.*

Education and Professional Life

- The late Michel Cineus, church director and preacher at Notre Dame of Lourdes Catholic Chapel of Gros-Saut, Leogane, Haiti, for allowing me to preach at the chapel during my teenage years.

- Professor Frantz Theodat, who taught me the invaluable role a mentor plays in professional development and success.

- Jean Paul Faubert, who helped open the doors to my education journey in America.

- The late Father Claude Chenier, who introduced me to the power of positive thinking and supported my early artistic and leadership endeavors.

- The late Father Charles Benoit, whose preaching skills inspired my speaking mission.

- The group "Sainte Famille" (Holy Family) of Saint Bernadette Catholic Church in Port-au-Prince, Haiti, which introduced me to public speaking at the age of eleven.

- Gilbert Louis-Jacques, my cousin, along with his wife and his sisters-in-law, who graciously welcomed me into their home in 1987.

- Mrs. Hermite Massenat, my former Hermann Heraux Elementary School dean, who ignited my passion for success when I was 11 years old.

- The mentors from my neighborhood of Cite Macoute, Port-au-Prince, Haiti: Fritz Charles, Evans Damis, and Jean-Kelly Damis, who mentored me as a student and constantly showed their belief in my skills and my potential for success.

- The members of ALAEN, Martissant, Port-au-Prince, Haiti, the former literary and artistic youth group, with whom I developed my communication, writing, performing, and speaking skills.

- Astrid Sanchez, my advisor at Edmonds College, who facilitated my technology education, which has been significant in my professional achievements.

- Marion Weldon, my former business instructor and current career-life transformational consultant, who proudly earned the title of book writing coach for this book. From Mrs. Marion, I learned the importance of having a life mission at Edmonds College in Lynnwood, Washington.

- Motivational speaker and author Jack Canfield, who strengthened my knowledge on the concepts of life mission and goal setting through his video program titled *Self-Esteem and Peak Performance*.

- Dr. Anel Monrose, who referred me to one of my most significant professional career opportunities.

- Chelsea St Cyr, who has helped complete the book project in her multi-faceted role of book coach, graphic designer, and editor-in-chief. Thanks a million, Chelsea.

- My beloved former classmates from Promotion Soleil of College Canado-Haitien High School, Port-au-Prince, Haiti, including the "Manistes": Lespinasse Leveille, Michel-Ange Zamor, Jean-Raymond Homere, and Patrick Morisseau, who not only reinforced my belief in the value of thinking big but also exemplified the courage and boldness needed to pursue our dreams. Their unwavering support and friendship have been a source of inspiration and love throughout my journey.

- The board members, members, and sponsors of Promotion Soleil Inc., an alumni organization of my Class of 1982-1989 of College Canado-Haitien High School across the USA, Canada, and Haiti, whose primary mission is to improve the lives of the less fortunate in the communities they serve.

- Andre Rosier and the members of Alfa Tanboula Organization, which promoted the literacy movement in Haiti through Haitian Creole publications and cultural events.

- François Joachin Dessalines, CEO of SHARE, a U.S.-based charity organization helping children in Haiti, who has always promoted my speaking career.

- Jean-Marie Etswald Ligondé, whose advice to urgently author a book to succeed as a motivational speaker I took to heart and made a reality. Thank you so much for your words of motivation.

- Takeo Uchiyama, former student advisor for Japanese students at Edmonds College, who has always supported my endeavors and contributed his ideas, helping me understand the Ikigai concept for completing the corresponding section in the book.

- Dr. Alix Charles, whose support has been unwavering for all my projects and who represents an invaluable partner.

- Dixon Alexandre, who remains a priceless partner and has always supported my philanthropic endeavors in Haiti, especially the development projects of Gros-Saut in Leogane, Haiti.

- Diane Shiner of Seattle, Washington, who proudly earned the title of best host mother in America; her three daughters; and my two kind roommates, Sylvain Bernard and Risa Baba.

- The professional team of Trait d'Union Radio Show of WSRF 1580 AM Radio Station of South Florida, which has been supporting me for the past six years.

- My partners and friends in the medical field, including administrative and customer service staff, the media, and the community organizations of South Florida
- Dr. Flore Lindor Latortue, founder and host of Radio TV and CEO of Gade Tet Ou. LLC, whose unwavering support is noteworthy.
- All my instructors and professors from pre-K to graduate school, each of whom has placed a brick in my achievement pyramid.

- All my customers in the insurance industry, who often make me feel more like a personal coach and family member than a service provider.

To all my friends and everyone who has contributed to my enriching life journey, each of you has played a part in this monumental project in ways that are beyond words. I am convinced there are unsung heroes I could not mention. This book is as much yours as it is mine. Thank you for being part of the melody of my life story.

References

"Albert Einstein Quotes." BrainyQuote.com. BrainyMedia Inc, 2024. Accessed May 4, 2024. https://www.brainyquote.com/quotes/albert_einstein_1 22232.

Barker, Joel A. "Joel A. Barker Quotes." BrainyQuote. Accessed October 29, 2023. https://www.brainyquote.com/quotes/joel_a_barker_15 8200.

BBC News. "Greta Thunberg: The Swedish Teen Who Became the Voice of Climate Change Activism." BBC News, December 11, 2019. Accessed May 17, 2024. https://www.bbc.com/news/world-europe-50740324.

Brunon, Georges. *L'art et le Vivant [Art and Life]*. Saint-Jean-de-Braye: Éditions de l'Art Vivant, 1982.

Canfield, Jack. *Self-Esteem and Peak Performance*. 1987. Internet Archive. Accessed June 26, 2024. https://archive.org/details/self-esteem-and-peak-performance-jack-canfield-1987-tapes.

Cleveland Clinic. "Transcendental Meditation." Cleveland Clinic. Accessed March 18, 2024. https://my.clevelandclinic.org/health/treatments/22292 -transcendental-meditation.

Dalai Lama. "In order to carry a positive action, we must develop here a positive vision." BrainyQuote. Accessed October 29, 2023. https://www.brainyquote.com/quotes/dalai_lama_4467 40.

Doran, George T. "There's a S.M.A.R.T. Way to Write Management's Goals and Objectives." *Management Review* 70, no. 11 (1981): 35-36.

Fabry, Joseph B. "The Pursuit of Meaning." Purpose Research (2013).

Forbes Health. "Blue Zones in the US: What Are They and Why Are They Important?" Forbes, March 6, 2024. Accessed May 17, 2024. https://www.forbes.com/health/nutrition/blue-zones-in-the-us/#:~:text=Simply%20put%2C%20blue%20zones%20are,term%20blue%20zones%20in%202004.

Frankl, Viktor E. Man's Search for Meaning. Boston: Beacon Press, 2006.

García, Héctor, and Francesc Miralles. Ikigai: The Japanese Secret to a Long and Happy Life. New York: Penguin Books, 2016.

Humphrey, Albert S. *SWOT Analysis*. Stanford Research Institute, 1970.

Imbastoni, Giulia. "What Is a Personal Vision Statement?" BetterUp. Accessed April 21, 2024.

https://www.betterup.com/blog/create-a-personal-
vision-statement#what-is-a-personal-vision-statement.

Lang, Andrew. The Story of Joan of Arc. Urbana, IL: Project
Gutenberg, 2015. Accessed March 25, 2020.
http://www.gutenberg.org/files/48470/48470-h/48470-
h.htm.

Perry, Elizabeth. "How to Create a Vision Board." BetterUp.
Accessed April 21, 2024.
https://www.betterup.com/blog/how-to-create-vision-
board.

PositivePsychology.com. "Positive Psychology: An
Introduction, Summary & PDF." Accessed June 11,
2024. https://positivepsychology.com/positive-
psychology-introduction-summary-pdf/.

"Self-discipline." In Collins English Dictionary. Accessed
April 23, 2024.
https://www.collinsdictionary.com/dictionary/english/s
elf-discipline.

The Ethics Centre. "Existentialism Explainer." Accessed
January 31, 2024. https://ethics.org.au/ethics-
explainer-
existentialism/#:~:text=Existentialism%20is%20the%2
0philosophical%20belief,governments%2C%20teacher
s%20or%20other%20authorities.

"Thomas A. Edison Quotes." BrainyQuote.com. BrainyMedia
Inc, 2023. Accessed December 18, 2023.

https://www.brainyquote.com/quotes/thomas_a_edison_131294.

Three Principles Foundation. "Genesis of the Three Principles." Accessed June 2, 2024. https://threeprinciplesfoundation.org/genesis-three-principles/.

"Focus." In Merriam-Webster.com Dictionary. Accessed April 23, 2024. https://www.merriam-webster.com/dictionary/focus.

WebMD. "What Is Logotherapy?" Accessed January 31, 2024. https://www.webmd.com/mental-health/what-is-logotherapy.

"Zig Ziglar Quotes." BrainyQuote.com. BrainyMedia Inc, 2023. Accessed December 18, 2023. https://www.brainyquote.com/quotes/zig_ziglar_617742.

"Zig Ziglar Quotes." BrainyQuote.com. BrainyMedia Inc, 2024. Accessed April 24, 2024. https://www.brainyquote.com/quotes/zig_ziglar_381983.

Suggested References

Bertolucci, Domonique. *Less Is More: 101 Ways to Simplify Your Life*. 3rd ed. Richmond: Hardie Grant Books, 2021.

Brown, Brené. *Daring Greatly: How the Courage to Be Vulnerable Transforms the Way We Live, Love, Parent, and Lead*. New York: Gotham Books, 2012.

Carnegie, Dale. *How to Win Friends and Influence People*. New York: Simon and Schuster, 2009.

Clear, James. *Atomic Habits: An Easy & Proven Way to Build Good Habits & Break Bad Ones*. New York: Avery, 2018.

Covey, Stephen R. *The 7 Habits of Highly Effective People: Powerful Lessons in Personal Change*. New York: Free Press, 2004.

Duckworth, Angela. *Grit: The Power of Passion and Perseverance*. New York: Scribner, 2016.

Dweck, Carol S. *Mindset: The New Psychology of Success*. New York: Random House, 2006.

Ferriss, Tim. *Tools of Titans: The Tactics, Routines, and Habits of Billionaires, Icons, and World-Class Performers*. Boston: Houghton Mifflin Harcourt, 2016.

Gladwell, Malcolm. *Outliers: The Story of Success*. New York: Little, Brown and Company, 2008.

Hill, Napoleon. *Think and Grow Rich*. New York: TarcherPerigee, 2007.

Keller, Gary, and Jay Papasan. *The One Thing: The Surprisingly Simple Truth Behind Extraordinary Results*. Austin: Bard Press, 2013.

McKeown, Greg. *Essentialism: The Disciplined Pursuit of Less*. New York: Crown Business, 2014.

Pink, Daniel H. *Drive: The Surprising Truth About What Motivates Us*. New York: Riverhead Books, 2009.

Ries, Eric. *The Lean Startup: How Today's Entrepreneurs Use Continuous Innovation to Create Radically Successful Businesses*. New York: Crown Business, 2011.

Robbins, Tony. *Awaken the Giant Within: How to Take Immediate Control of Your Mental, Emotional, Physical and Financial Destiny!*. New York: Free Press, 1991.

Ruiz, Don Miguel. *The Four Agreements: A Practical Guide to Personal Freedom*. San Rafael, CA: Amber-Allen Publishing, 1997.

Schwartz, David J. *The Magic of Thinking Big*. New York: Simon and Schuster, 2015.Sincero, Jen. *You Are a Badass: How to Stop Doubting Your Greatness and Start Living an Awesome Life*. Philadelphia: Running Press, 2013.

Sinek, Simon. *Start with Why: How Great Leaders Inspire Everyone to Take Action*. New York: Portfolio, 2009.

Spittle, Elsie, and Chip Chipman. *The Genesis of the Three Principles*. Amazon Kindle Direct Publishing, 2019.

Tolle, Eckhart. *The Power of Now: A Guide to Spiritual Enlightenment*. Novato, CA: New World Library, 1999.

www.ingramcontent.com/pod-product-compliance
Lightning Source LLC
Chambersburg PA
CBHW031142160726
47991CB00004B/1528